MW01289612

Book Two Of The "Heaven Now" Series

I Will Awaken The Dawn

Propiv Press
Lancaster Pennsylvania, USA

I Will Awaken The Dawn

By Jonathan Brenneman

I Will Awaken The Dawn

General Editor Arnolda M. Brenneman
Contributing Editor John Lee

Propiv Press, Lancaster, Pennsylvania, USA

ISBN-13: 978-1537649023
ISBN-10: 1537649027

Printed in the United States of America.

Dedication

I dedicate this work to Betsie Ten Boom and to every other believer who has learned to give thanks to God and live as a heavenly person regardless of earthly circumstances. Let's awaken the dawn!

Book Two in the "Heaven Now" trilogy

I Will Awaken The Dawn

Table of Contents

1. Earth Becoming Like Heaven

Belize

I went on my first trip to Belize when I was seventeen years old. It was a mission trip with a group from my church. We worked with a local pastor who had planted several churches around the country.

Belize is a tiny country in Central America. To the north is Mexico, to the west is Guatemala, and to the south is Honduras. It's the most sparsely populated country in Latin America, and the only one in which the primary language is English. However, almost half the people speak an English Creole, and over half of the people also speak Spanish.

I fell in love with the people, as I have in nearly every country I've visited. I especially loved playing with the children. They were wonderful! I felt like I fit in since I had learned to speak Spanish as a teenager.

The Belizean pastor invited me to come back, and I returned one year later. It was my first solo international trip. I ended up taking five or six trips to Belize, and I gained much scriptural understanding about praise and thanksgiving during this period of time.

Can Nations Be Saved?

As a teenager, I spent considerable time reading the Bible because I wanted to live my life 100% for the Lord's purposes. While going through the Old Testament, I lingered long in Psalms and Isaiah. These two books frequently talk about God's purposes for the nations.

I had previously read several accounts of historical and modern-day revivals. Psalms and Isaiah further inspired me to believe God for the transformation of nations through the truth of the gospel. I wanted to live my life for this purpose. Here are a few of those scriptures.

Psalm 2:8 Ask of me, and I will make the nations your heritage, and the ends of the earth your possession.

Psalm 22:27 All the ends of the earth shall remember and turn to the Lord; and all the families of the nations shall worship before him.

Ps. 86:9 All the nations you have made shall come and bow down before you, O Lord, and shall glorify your name.

Isaiah 52:10 The Lord has bared his holy arm before the eyes of all the nations; and all the ends of the earth shall see the salvation of our God.

Isaiah 60:3 Nations shall come to your light, and kings to the brightness of your dawn.

I began to pray for Belize during my first trip. As I prayed, I was suddenly overwhelmed with emotion and began to weep and cry out loudly.

I longed to see the very culture of this country influenced by the gospel. I imagined the crime rate plummeting and people everywhere talking about God's mighty works. I imagined thousands of people coming to Christ and being delivered from oppression. If this was possible, it was worth giving myself fully to the Lord for this purpose.

As I fasted and prayed, I felt the weight of the darkness over the nation of Belize. The prayer seemed to drain all my strength until I was exhausted.

Then the Lord spoke to me about praise and thanksgiving. Everywhere I looked, scriptures about praise jumped off the pages at me. On my second trip to Belize, all of these scriptures seemed to come together in my understanding. The Holy Spirit told me that the darkness and oppression I'd felt weighing on me was a lie, and I needed to cast it off. The Lord wanted me to see another reality— that Belize was filled with his glory.

The Earth Is Filled With The Lord's Glory, So Why Isn't It Just Like Heaven?

I wrote these books as a series for a reason. Understanding the concepts in the first book is necessary to follow my train of thought in the other two books. In *Present Access To Heaven* I made a case that heaven is heaven simply because God is there. The glory of God creates the reality of heaven.

Psalm 16:11 In your presence there is fullness of joy; in your right hand are pleasures forevermore.

Several scriptures state that the whole earth is full of the glory of the Lord. I understand *"the earth is full of God's steadfast love"* to be synonymous with *"the earth is full of God's glory."*

Psalm 33:5 He loves righteousness and justice; the earth is full of the steadfast love of the Lord.

Psalm 119:64 The earth, O Lord, is full of your steadfast love.

Isaiah 6:3 And one called to another and said: "Holy, holy, holy is the Lord of hosts; the whole earth is full of his glory."

As I read through Psalms and Isaiah, I wondered *"If heaven is heaven because of God's glory, and the whole earth is full of God's glory, then why isn't the earth just like heaven?"*

The Earth Will Be Full Of The Knowledge Of The Lord's Glory

One day, while reading the Bible, I caught a significant detail previously unnoticed. Scripture says the earth is *presently* full of the glory of the Lord, but it *will be full* of the knowledge of his glory. What's the difference?

Habbakuk 2:14 But the earth will be filled with the knowledge of the glory of the Lord, as the waters cover the sea.

I began to notice the concept of *"the knowledge of the Lord"* found repeatedly in scripture. It seemed like it was everywhere! In *Present Access To Heaven* I wrote extensively on this. We saw that *"the knowledge of the Lord"* can be equated with salvation. It speaks of experience with God and participation in his nature.

In Belize, I learned that anywhere we are is heaven because the earth is full of God's glory. Yet we only experience heaven when our eyes are opened to see God's glory that fills the earth!

Our eyes need to be opened! Mankind has been blinded to the glory of the Lord filling the earth.

1. Earth Becoming Like Heaven

Scripture describes what it will look like when the whole earth is full of *the knowledge* of the Lord's glory.

Isaiah 11:6-9 The wolf shall live with the lamb, the leopard shall lie down with the kid, the calf and the lion and the fatling together, and a little child shall lead them. The cow and the bear shall graze, their young shall lie down together; and the lion shall eat straw like the ox. The nursing child shall play over the hole of the asp, and the weaned child shall put its hand on the adder's den. They will not hurt or destroy on all my holy mountain; for the earth will be full of the knowledge of the Lord as the waters cover the sea.

Isaiah 2:2-4 In days to come the mountain of the Lord's house shall be established as the highest of the mountains, and shall be raised above the hills; all the nations shall stream to it. Many peoples shall come and say, "Come, let us go up to the mountain of the Lord, to the house of the God of Jacob; that he may teach us his ways and that we may walk in his paths." For out of Zion shall go forth instruction, and the word of the Lord from Jerusalem. He shall judge between the nations, and shall arbitrate for many peoples; they shall beat their swords into plowshares, and their spears into pruning hooks; nation shall not lift up sword against nation, neither shall they learn war any more.

Earth will become like heaven when it's filled with the knowledge of the Lord's glory! So what part can we play in bringing this about?

2. The Dawn

Thick Darkness Covers The Peoples

Isaiah describes a *"thick darkness"* that covers the nations. Yet a dawn of the Lord's light will rise over the peoples of the earth.

Isaiah 60:1-3 Arise, shine; for your light has come, and the glory of the LORD has risen upon you. For darkness shall cover the earth, and thick darkness the peoples; but the LORD will arise upon you, and his glory will appear over you. Nations shall come to your light, and kings to the brightness of your dawn.

The substance of this *"thick darkness"* is lies. It is deception which keeps people from seeing God's glory which fills the earth. This was the heaviness I felt over Belize, and which the Lord told me to cast off. I was to cast it off, recognizing it as a lie, because the reality is that Belize is full of the glory of the Lord! I was to put on the *"garment of praise"* for the *"spirit of heaviness."*

Isaiah 61:3 (NKJV) To console those who mourn in Zion, To give them beauty for ashes, The oil of joy for mourning, The garment of praise for the spirit of heaviness; That they may be called trees of righteousness, The planting of the LORD, that He may be glorified.

Using various terminologies, many other scriptures refer to the *"thick darkness"* of Isaiah 60. It is the *"spirit of heaviness"* in Isaiah 61. It is the *"veil"* that keeps people from seeing the light of God's glory in the face of Christ. Satan is a liar, and the father of lies.[1]

2 Corinthians 4:3-6 And even if our gospel is veiled, it is veiled to those who are perishing. In their case the god of this world has blinded the minds of the unbelievers, to keep them from seeing the light of the gospel of the glory of Christ, who is the image of God. For we do not proclaim ourselves; we proclaim Jesus Christ as Lord and ourselves as your slaves for Jesus' sake. For it is the God who said, "Let light shine out of darkness," who has shone in our hearts to give the light of the knowledge of the glory of God in the face of Jesus Christ.

Isaiah 25:6-10 On this mountain the Lord of hosts will make for all peoples a feast of rich food, a feast of well-aged wines, of rich food filled with marrow, of well-aged wines strained clear. And he will destroy on this mountain the shroud that is cast over all peoples, the sheet that is spread over all nations; he will swallow up death forever.

Then the Lord God will wipe away the tears from all faces, and the disgrace of his people he will take away from all the earth, for the Lord has spoken. It will be said on that day, Lo, this is our God; we have waited for him, so that he might save us. This is the Lord for whom we have waited; let us be glad and rejoice in his salvation. For the hand of the Lord will rest on this mountain.

---

[1] John 8:44

Declare God's Praise To The Nations

As I prayed for Belize and read these scriptures, I came across this passage, which we find in both Psalm 57 and Psalm 108.

Psalm 51:7-11, Psalm 108:1-5 My heart is steadfast, O God, my heart is steadfast. I will sing and make melody. Awake, my soul! Awake, O harp and lyre! I will awake the dawn. I will give thanks to you, O Lord, among the peoples; I will sing praises to you among the nations.

For your steadfast love is as high as the heavens; your faithfulness extends to the clouds. Be exalted, O God, above the heavens. Let your glory be over all the earth.

I had read the description in Isaiah 60 of a dawning of the light of God's glory over the earth, so that thick darkness would no longer cover the nations. In Psalms and in Isaiah, I read one scripture after another about praise and nations turning to God. Then I came to this passage about *"awakening the dawn."* The context was thanksgiving and declaring God's praise.

Could it be that we could *"awaken the dawn,"* described in Isaiah 60, by giving thanks to God and declaring his praise? I believed this was what the Holy Spirit was showing me, and also what scripture was pointing to.

How did this *"thick darkness"* come to be in the first place? Look at how Romans describes the fall of man and the descent of darkness over the earth:

Romans 1:21 (GW) They knew God but did not praise and thank him for being God. Instead, their thoughts were pointless, and their misguided minds were plunged into darkness.

Romans 1:21 (NIV) For although they knew God, they neither glorified him as God nor gave thanks to him, but their thinking became futile and their foolish hearts were darkened.

Darkness came over the minds and hearts of mankind as they failed to praise and thank him. This is how people who knew God became blinded to the light of his glory. Doesn't it make sense that we would awaken the dawn of the knowledge of the Lord's glory again, as we give praise and thanks to God?

Here are some of the scriptures I read about singing God's praise and God's dominion in the nations of the earth. These scriptures triggered supernatural experiences for me as I continued to meditate on them, and so I share them with you.

Psalm 47:1-9 Clap your hands, all you peoples; shout to God with loud songs of joy. For the LORD, the Most High, is awesome, a great king over all the earth. He subdued peoples under us, and nations under our feet. He chose our heritage for us, the pride of Jacob whom he loves. Selah

God has gone up with a shout, the LORD with the sound of a trumpet. Sing praises to God, sing praises; sing praises to our King, sing praises. For God is the king of all the earth; sing praises with a psalm. God is king over the nations; God sits on his holy throne. The princes of the peoples gather as the people of the God of Abraham. For the shields of the earth belong to God; he is highly exalted.

Psalm 9:11 Sing praises to the LORD, who dwells in Zion. Declare his deeds among the peoples.

2. The Dawn

Psalm 18:49 For this I will extol you, O LORD, among the nations, and sing praises to your name.

Psalm 66:1-4 Make a joyful noise to God, all the earth; sing the glory of his name; give to him glorious praise. Say to God, "How awesome are your deeds! Because of your great power, your enemies cringe before you. All the earth worships you; they sing praises to you, sing praises to your name." Selah

Psalm 117 Praise the Lord, all you nations! Extol him, all you peoples! For great is his steadfast love toward us, and the faithfulness of the Lord endures forever. Praise the Lord!

Psalm 67:1-7 (KJV) God be merciful unto us, and bless us; and cause his face to shine upon us; Selah. That thy way may be known upon earth, thy saving health among all nations.

Let the people praise thee, O God; let all the people praise thee. O let the nations be glad and sing for joy: for thou shalt judge the people righteously, and govern the nations upon earth. Selah.

Let the people praise thee, O God; let all the people praise thee. Then shall the earth yield her increase; and God, even our own God, shall bless us. God shall bless us; and all the ends of the earth shall fear him.

What a tremendous promise we see in Psalm 67! All nations and peoples shall praise the Lord, and then the earth will yield its increase. All the ends of the earth will fear the Lord.

We see in scripture that when people praised the Lord and declared his goodness, the place was filled with a cloud of glory. They couldn't even remain standing under this powerful and tangible manifestation of heaven. We know from scripture that the place where they were was already filled with God's glory before they began to sing his praise. Yet as they declared God's goodness, the place was filled with the knowledge of the glory of the Lord and became like heaven.

2 Chronicles 5:12-14 ...all the levitical singers, Asaph, Heman, and Jeduthun, their sons and kindred, arrayed in fine linen, with cymbals, harps, and lyres, stood east of the altar with one hundred twenty priests who were trumpeters. It was the duty of the trumpeters and singers to make themselves heard in unison in praise and thanksgiving to the Lord, and when the song was raised, with trumpets and cymbals and other musical instruments, in praise to the Lord,
"For he is good, for his steadfast love endures forever,"
the house, the house of the Lord, was filled with a cloud, so that the priests could not stand to minister because of the cloud; for the glory of the Lord filled the house of God.

When the people praised the Lord, it wasn't only the ones singing praise whose eyes were opened to see God's glory. His glory became manifest so that everybody could see it. They awoke the dawn of the knowledge of the Lord's glory in that place.

God's glory fills the whole earth. If we can see the Lord's glory wherever we are, that place becomes heaven to us. This is true no matter how dark that place may seem. As we see God's glory and our mouths are filled with praise and declaration of his goodness, our environments can be filled with the knowledge of the glory of the Lord so that *everybody* can see it. The thick darkness blinding people's eyes to the light of God's glory is removed.

"I Will Sing Your Praise Before The Gods"

Read these scriptures carefully. As you read, pay special attention to what they say about praising the Lord before false gods.

Psalm 138:1-2 I give you thanks, O Lord, with my whole heart; before the gods I sing your praise; I bow down toward your holy temple and give thanks to your name for your steadfast love and your faithfulness

Psalm 96:1-13 O sing to the Lord a new song; sing to the Lord, all the earth. Sing to the Lord, bless his name; tell of his salvation from day to day. Declare his glory among the nations, his marvelous works among all the peoples.

For great is the Lord, and greatly to be praised; he is to be revered above all gods. For all the gods of the peoples are idols, but the Lord made the heavens. Honor and majesty are before him; strength and beauty are in his sanctuary.

Ascribe to the Lord, O families of the peoples, ascribe to the Lord glory and strength. Ascribe to the Lord the glory due his name; bring an offering, and come into his courts. Worship the Lord in holy splendor; tremble before him, all the earth.

Say among the nations, "The Lord is king! The world is firmly established; it shall never be moved. He will judge the peoples with equity." Let the heavens be glad, and let the earth rejoice; let the sea roar, and all that fills it; let the field exult, and everything in it.

Then shall all the trees of the forest sing for joy before the Lord; for he is coming, for he is coming to judge the earth. He will judge the world with righteousness, and the peoples with his truth.

The Lord showed me that I was too impressed with false gods. I felt such heaviness as I prayed for Belize because I was so preoccupied with what the devil was doing that it clouded my vision of the Lord. The spirit of violence, the spirit of addiction, the spirit of immorality, and other forms of evil at work in Belize were far bigger in my perception than they should have been. I was over-impressed with them. They were false gods, and I was not to give them any honor.

How was I honoring them, since I was praying against them? They had become bigger in the eyes of my heart than the glory of God, which scripture says fills the whole earth, and which therefore fills Belize. Fullness of joy is found in the Lord's presence, so if my attention is in the right place I should have fullness of joy. Why should any power of evil be bigger in the eyes of my heart than the reality of God's glory which fills the earth?

We often think of idolatry as loving something more than the Lord. But how often do we think of idolatry as fearing something more than the Lord? If you take time to look at images of idols, it's clear that many of them are designed to capture our attention through fear. Shadrach, Meshach, and Abednego were not tempted to bow down to King Nebuchadnezzar's golden statue by loving it more than they loved the Lord. Rather, they were tempted to fear it more than they feared the Lord.

It was only because I beheld false gods that heaviness filled my heart rather than the fullness of joy that's in the Lord's presence. The heaviness was a lie, because all the works of the devil in this country were nothing compared to the Lord and his glory. I was giving the attention that only God deserved to the devil. I was to only be impressed with the Lord, and not to fear any other.

In *Present Access To Heaven* I shared a few stories of people getting hurt when they decided to assault a demonic principality. I concluded their error was attempting to *"pull down"* the principality, as if they were under it. Their attention became focused on the false god they were attempting to displace, instead of on the Lord and his glory. It was actually idolatry! I was making the same mistake.

The Lord showed me that if I began to turn the eyes of my heart towards him with praise and thanksgiving, I would see his glory that fills Belize, and Belize would become heaven to me. I was to sing the Lord's praise before the gods.

I was to behold the glory of the Lord which filled my surroundings, and then continually declare what I was seeing. Psalm 97 showed me what I should expect to happen as I declared the Lord's praise before all false gods.

Psalm 97:1-8 The Lord is king! Let the earth rejoice; let the many coastlands be glad! Clouds and thick darkness are all around him; righteousness and justice are the foundation of his throne.

Fire goes before him, and consumes his adversaries on every side. His lightnings light up the world; the earth sees and trembles.

The mountains melt like wax before the Lord, before the Lord of all the earth. The heavens proclaim his righteousness; and all the peoples behold his glory.

All worshipers of images are put to shame, those who make their boast in worthless idols; all gods bow down before him. Zion hears and is glad and the towns of Judah rejoice, because of your judgments, O God. For you, O Lord, are most high over all the earth; you are exalted far above all gods.

The priests could no longer stand to minister because of the manifestation of God's presence when they sang his praise. Likewise, I could expect a tangible manifestation of the Lord's glory that would cause the mountains of evil which seemed so big to melt like wax. I would turn up the heat by giving praise and thanks to God.

I saw that all peoples will behold the glory of the Lord, because the earth will be filled with the knowledge of the Lord's glory. I was going to do my part in bringing this about.

Psalm 105:1-5 O give thanks to the Lord, call on his name, make known his deeds among the peoples. Sing to him, sing praises to him; tell of all his wonderful works. Glory in his holy name; let the hearts of those who seek the Lord rejoice. Seek the Lord and his strength; seek his presence continually. Remember the wonderful works he has done, his miracles, and the judgments he has uttered...

I began to connect the dots between these scriptures around the time of my second trip to Belize. When the Lord told me to throw off the heaviness I felt, I obeyed. I refused to be impressed any longer with anything that the devil had done in this country. I chose to fix my attention on the Lord's glory that already filled Belize.

Orange Walk Town

I remember riding from the west part of the country to the northern part in the back of a pickup truck. The pastor who invited me had recently planted a church in a town called Orange Walk.

I'd heard about Orange Walk. People told me it was dangerous. A lot of gang members operated there. To a person seeing with only human eyes, it looked like a dark place.

I met a young man whose upper body was covered with scars. He had been walking in Orange Walk and met some guys who made fun of his girlfriend. When he said *"Hey guys, leave her alone,"* they attacked him with knives and machetes. They stabbed him multiple times, and he had slash marks from machetes going all the way across his back.

He was left on the ground and cried out to God to help him and save his life. He told the Lord that if his life was saved, he would repent from his rebellion and stop using drugs. Then, finding strength to get to someone who could help him, he collapsed on the ground in front of their door.

Within three days he had recovered enough strength to play volleyball. I was amazed! I saw the scars covering his back and stomach. Such a recovery could be nothing less than miraculous!

Orange Walk seemed like a dark and dangerous place, but I knew it was filled with God's glory. The back of the pickup truck was a great place to pray and sing to the Lord. Going 60 miles an hour down the highway, the wind was so loud that nobody heard me.

I remembered every time the Lord had saved me, helped me, and delivered me. I wept as I began to thank him, and truly began to feel like I was in heaven. My heart was bursting with power. I wanted to shout. I felt like rivers of God's love were flowing through me, and that love was so powerful that nothing was impossible.

When I arrived at Orange Walk, I had a good time hanging out and talking with people. Yet I felt that I couldn't stop thanking the Lord. The whole time, I quietly gave thanks and praise to God. I was singing in tongues without even thinking about it.

Psalm 34:1 I will bless the Lord at all times; his praise shall continually be in my mouth.

The love I felt for everybody around me overwhelmed me. I didn't just love the people, but I even loved the trees and everything else. It felt like everything around me was vibrating with the goodness of God.

There was a church meeting that night, under a tarp in the open air. About 30 people gathered. As the worship team practiced, I sat in the back singing to the Lord and talking to people. I felt like my face had become radiant, glowing with the light of the Lord's glory which I saw.

As we sang and gave thanks to God during the meeting, I began to shout. It was almost involuntary, coming from the very depths of my being. The joy and thankfulness I felt towards the Lord for saving me could not be expressed in words.

Psalm 32:7 You are a hiding place for me; you preserve me from trouble; you surround me with glad cries of deliverance. Selah

Psalm 32:11 Be glad in the Lord and rejoice, O righteous, and shout for joy, all you upright in heart.

I knew about the drug dealing, the violence, and the crime in Orange Walk. But I now saw that it was filled with the glory of God, and it was heaven. As I came into the knowledge of the Lord's glory, I began to feel my body physically vibrating with God's goodness. It felt like a weight over me and a love so strong it was tangible. I could barely stand on my feet.

In that moment, I realized that nothing was impossible. I saw the Lord, and he was so much bigger than anything else that had captured my attention. He was so much more impressive than any evil spirit which had caused destruction in Orange Walk.

I began to declare what I saw. I proclaimed that the people in Orange Walk would encounter God and be delivered. I pronounced that the veil which kept people from seeing the glory of God in the face of Christ, would be removed. Orange Walk would no longer be covered in thick darkness, but the people would sing God's praise on the streets! Orange Walk and Belize would be filled with shouts of joy and glad cries of deliverance!

By the end of that meeting, I had a radically different perspective. I couldn't see any difference from a natural viewpoint, but the eyes of my heart had been opened and Orange Walk was now heaven to me. I saw that Orange Walk was filled with God's glory. I knew it.

Revival In Orange Walk!

About two months after I returned from that trip to Belize, I talked with a pastor who had just returned from his own trip there. He told me *"Revival broke out in Orange Walk! The church has more than doubled, and it's almost all people who just got saved!"*

This was what had happened since my experience in Orange Walk! I couldn't prove this had anything to do with my experience. But I was convinced that truths which I felt the Lord was showing me in scripture, about praise and thanksgiving, had just been practically demonstrated. Orange Walk began to be filled with the knowledge of the Lord's glory.

Most of these new believers in Orange Walk were teenagers or young adults in their twenties. I got to know many of them during later trips to Belize. They were so new to the Lord, and in need of discipleship! But they were so passionate! Since then, many of them have become evangelists, sharing the gospel in different parts of their country with evangelistic skits, Christian rap, dance, and other means.

All of Belize, and all of the earth, is filled with the glory of the Lord. Many people are still blind to that fact. But Belize, and every nation, will be filled with the knowledge of the Lord's glory, as the waters cover the seas! The veil, the thick darkness that has covered the nations, is being removed!

3. I Am In Heaven

I know the experience I've described is mystical. Yet it's scriptural. The Bible gives many accounts of people having an overwhelmingly powerful, tangible experience of the Lord's glory.

I began to have such tangible experiences of God's glory with increasing frequency. These experiences were often triggered as I began to thank and praise the Lord, or meditate on certain scriptures.

We've seen in Psalm 96 that even the trees of the forest sing for joy. Jesus said if the people stopped praising him, even the stones would shout out.[2] I think these scriptures are more than just figurative. Even the vibrations emitted by God's creation, which the human ear cannot detect, are praising the Lord.

Psalm 19:1-4 The heavens are telling the glory of God; and the firmament proclaims his handiwork. Day to day pours forth speech, and night to night declares knowledge. There is no speech, nor are there words; their voice is not heard; yet their voice goes out through all the earth, and their words to the end of the world.

Romans 1:20 Ever since the creation of the world his eternal power and divine nature, invisible though they are, have been understood and seen through the things he has made.

---

[2] Luke 19:40

I've shared only a few scriptures about praise and thanksgiving which impressed me on my second trip to Belize. There were many more! I saw scriptures everywhere confirming my Belize experiences. The other scriptures and principles I refer to through the rest of this book are also things I began to understand in Belize. They triggered my supernatural experience of experiencing heaven in Belize.

St. Petersburg

Another place I had such a tangible experience of heaven on earth was Saint Petersburg, Russia. I traveled to Russia for the first time with the youth group, not expecting I'd ever visit there again. Yet I somehow learned most of the Cyrillic alphabet on my second day there. By the end of the two week trip, I could read and understand the book of First John in Russian. (Although my pronunciation was poor.) I fell in love with the people, especially the Russian grandmothers.

On the last day, we left early in the morning to go to the airport. It was summertime, so the sun set around 2:00 a.m. and rose again in a few hours. I remember riding through the city in a van at 3:00 in the morning. I was awake and alert. Leaving was bittersweet.

I sang quietly to the Lord. I thanked him for what he'd done in my life, for the people I'd met in Russia, and for everything I'd experienced there. I started to physically feel a current of God's love flowing through my body and out of my mouth, then increasing in intensity. My mouth and hands began to vibrate.

I felt indescribable love. I loved the people, the city, even the buildings around me. It seemed as if even the buildings were singing praise to God. I moved my hands through the air and physically felt the glory of God around me, as if my hands were passing through water or some other substance. The air was thick with God's presence, and everything was singing his praise.

St. Petersburg is a city with a painful history. I talked with old women who told me the stories of Hitler's siege on St. Petersburg. (Called Leningrad at that time.) They had family members who starved to death. Much more suffering followed, under communism.

Yet St. Petersburg became heaven to me. As the Lord opened my spiritual eyes, I saw that this city was full of God's goodness. A time will come when St. Petersburg will be so filled with the knowledge of the glory of the Lord, that everyone will see his glory as I did. St. Petersburg will become like heaven to all, because when it's filled with the knowledge of the Lord's glory, no one will harm or destroy anymore. The love of God will reign in the hearts of men.

I believe scripture verifies that no matter what natural circumstances look like in a place, if our eyes are opened, that place will be heaven to us. You may feel this is a nice theory, but impossible in reality. You may think some cities are too dark for us to perceive them as heaven.

What I am saying is being tested in my life again, right now. I live near Rio de Janeiro, Brazil. Since I started writing this book, we and two of our neighbors got bullets in our houses. Violence, crime, and corruption are rampant. My wife has been at gunpoint more than once. Just a few years ago, there were tanks rolling down the streets of the city.

People are setting cars and busses on fire. I was teaching in downtown Rio and heard bombs exploding outside as people were rioting. The current president and the ex-president, as well as many other government officials, are now being investigated for corruption and money-laundering.

I have some friends a few blocks up the street who own a snack bar. Jesus healed several of them after I first met them. I visited them two weeks ago and was shocked to hear that they lost a little girl who was kidnapped and killed on the highway. I had no words.

Immediately after hearing about that tragic event, I laid hands on another member of their family in Jesus' name. God healed her. God's goodness remains constant and fills the earth no matter how horrible events or natural circumstances may be.

After that we learned that an 85-year old man whom we know was repeatedly robbed and attacked with a knife. Criminals were breaking in his house at night and threatening him. He could have easily been killed.

We took him in to protect him. The criminals got angry and threatened us, and we knew our lives could be in danger. One threatened to kidnap our daughter. The police don't offer any real protection where we live. Yet Rio de Janeiro is filled with the goodness and glory of God. Scripture says so.

There have been some difficult moments, and the drama has not ended yet. However, I know I am rich, because I have God's presence. Many people are praying for us, and I feel a strong sense of the Lord's peace. I'm in heaven.

Psalm 3:3-6 But you, O LORD, are a shield round me, my glory, and the one who lifts up my head. I cry aloud to the LORD, and he answers me from his holy hill. Selah

I lie down and sleep; I wake again, for the LORD sustains me. I am not afraid of ten thousands of people who have set themselves against me all around.

Psalm 27:3 Though an army encamp against me, my heart shall not fear; though war rise up against me, yet I will be confident.

It would be easy to curse the city where I reside. Yet I know that according to scripture, Rio de Janeiro and all of Brazil are filled with the God's glory. The Lord wants me to see from his perspective. I thank the Father for my city. I will bless the land in which I live until it is full of the knowledge of God's glory.

Proverbs 11:11 By the blessing of the upright a city is exalted, but it is overthrown by the mouth of the wicked.

Psalm 37:1-2, 9-11 Do not fret because of the wicked; do not be envious of wrongdoers, for they will soon fade like the grass, and wither like the green herb...For the wicked shall be cut off, but those who wait for the Lord shall inherit the land. Yet a little while, and the wicked will be no more; though you look diligently for their place, they will not be there. But the meek shall inherit the land, and delight themselves in abundant prosperity.

Enter His Gates With Thanksgiving

Psalm 100:4-5 Enter his gates with thanksgiving, and his courts with praise. Give thanks to him, bless his name. For the LORD is good; his steadfast love endures forever, and his faithfulness to all generations.

Psalm 95:1-2 O come, let us sing to the LORD; let us make a joyful noise to the rock of our salvation! Let us come into his presence with thanksgiving; let us make a joyful noise to him with songs of praise!

Some people feel that these verses are not applicable for us in the New Covenant, since God's presence dwells

25

within us and we are his temple. That is true. However, I would like to note that Hebrews still talks about our approaching the Lord. John, in the book of Revelation, was told to *"come up here."*[3]

Yes, we are already in the Lord's presence. Yet we become aware his presence as we approach him with praise and thanksgiving.

Even Hell On Earth Is Heaven If You Can See From God's Perspective

Psalm 139:7-12 Where can I go from your spirit? Or where can I flee from your presence? If I ascend to heaven, you are there; if I make my bed in Sheol, you are there. If I take the wings of the morning and settle at the farthest limits of the sea, even there your hand shall lead me, and your right hand shall hold me fast. If I say, "Surely the darkness shall cover me, and the light around me become night," even the darkness is not dark to you; the night is as bright as the day, for darkness is as light to you.

I love reading biographies of believers who've gone before me. Their stories confirm that what I'm saying isn't only a nice theory. We can experience heaven in even the most horrible of places when our eyes are opened to see the Lord's goodness filling the earth.

It's hard to imagine a worse place on earth than a communist dungeon and torture chamber. Yet Richard Wurmbrand experienced God's presence there, during his fourteen years in communist prisons. He said that in the darkest hours of torture, Jesus came to them, and his presence made the walls shine like diamonds and fill the cells with light!

---

[3] Revelation 4:1

It seemed like the torturers were somewhere far below, in the sphere of the body, while their spirits rejoiced in the Lord. Wurmbrand said he and the other prisoners wouldn't have given up such joy for that of kingly palaces![4]

Just as it seemed to me that even the buildings and trees were praising God, the prisons walls seemed to shine like diamonds to Wurmbrand. The darkness was as light to the Lord. Even the dungeon was filled with the glory of God.

Wurmbrand's experience demonstrates that any place can become like heaven to us as the eyes of our hearts are opened to see God's glory. He spoke of the torture often seeming distant and far-removed from his spirit, which was lost in God's presence and glory. He learned that the spirit is master of the body.[5]

Wurmbrand even said his time in prison was *"occasionally a very happy time."* Other prisoners and guards were amazed at how happy Christians could be in prison, singing and dancing for joy even though they were beaten for it.[6] How was it possible for anyone to have such joy in these horrible circumstances?

Wurmbrand and the other Christian prisoners couldn't be stopped from singing praise to God! They chose to awaken the dawn, singing the Lord's praise before the gods. The greatest of evils couldn't keep them from beholding the glory of the Lord! The weakness of those false gods was exposed and they lost much of their influence. Even in one of the darkest places on earth, the light of the knowledge of God's glory began to shine!

---

[4] Wurmbrand, Richard (2010-09-30). Tortured for Christ (Kindle Locations 1289-1291). Living Sacrifice Book Company. Kindle Edition.
[5] Wurmbrand, Richard (2010-09-30). Tortured for Christ (Kindle Locations 788-791). Living Sacrifice Book Company. Kindle Edition.
[6] Wurmbrand, Richard (2010-09-30). Tortured for Christ (Kindle Locations 1028-1033). Living Sacrifice Book Company. Kindle Edition.

The Iron Curtain soon fell, and without bloodshed! It was a miraculous event. Many people came to salvation. The light of the knowledge of God's glory dawned on the Soviet Block. It will surely increase until the whole earth is full of the knowledge of his glory.

Russia, Eastern Europe, and Central Asia, will become like heaven! The weapons of our warfare are not merely human, but are powerful to destroy strongholds![7]

Although they still have a way to go, these countries are not as oppressive as they previously were. Let's continue to proclaim God's praise to these nations and awaken the dawn!

Living in a Nazi Concentration camp is also a horrendous ordeal. Yet Corrie Ten Boom spoke of experiencing heaven there.

At last either Betsie or I would open the Bible. Because only the Hollanders could understand the Dutch text, we would translate aloud in German. And then we would hear the life-giving words passed back along the aisles in French, Polish, Russian, Czech, back into Dutch. They were little previews of heaven, these evenings beneath the lightbulb.[8]

If Nazi prisoners could experience heaven in a concentration camp, and Soviet prisoners could see the glory of God filling a torture chamber, then it must be possible for me to experience heaven in any place I go!

Oh, that the eyes of our hearts would be opened! Give us your perspective God. Let's sing the Lord's praise before all false gods! Let's declare God's glory to the nations!

---

[7] 2 Corinthians 10:4
[8] Boom, Corrie Ten; Elizabeth Sherrill; John Sherrill (2006-01-01). The Hiding Place (pp. 212-213). Baker Publishing Group. Kindle Edition.

4. Proclamation

Adding Our "Amen" To God's "Yes"

One theme we see throughout scripture is that God's word is powerful. God created the world by his word, and he continues to accomplish his will by sending forth his word.

Hebrews 11:3 By faith we understand that the worlds were prepared by the word of God, so that what is seen was made from things that are not visible.

Hebrews 1:3 He is the reflection of God's glory and the exact imprint of God's very being, and he sustains all things by his powerful word.

James 1:18 In fulfillment of his own purpose he gave us birth by the word of truth, so that we would become a kind of first fruits of his creatures.

Psalm 107:20 He sent out his word and healed them, and delivered them from destruction.

Psalm 147:15 He sends out his command to the earth; his word runs swiftly.

Isaiah 55:10-11 For as the rain and the snow come down from heaven, and do not return there until they have watered the earth, making it bring forth and sprout, giving seed to the sower and bread to the eater, so shall my word be that goes out from my mouth; it shall not return to me empty, but it shall accomplish that which I purpose, and succeed in the thing for which I sent it.

Jeremiah 1:12 ...I am watching over my word to perform it.

Scripture shows us a partnership between God and man. I will expound on this in the third volume of this series, *Jesus Has Come In The Flesh*. For now, it's sufficient to say that God has given authority to men, and miracles happen when men speak God's words!

Job 22:28 (NASB) You will also decree a thing, and it will be established for you; And light will shine on your ways.

Job 22:28 (VOICE) You will pronounce something to be, and He will make it so; light will break out across all of your paths.

2 Corinthians 1:19-20 For the Son of God, Jesus Christ, whom we proclaimed among you, Silvanus and Timothy and I, was not "Yes and No"; but in him it is always "Yes." For in him every one of God's promises is a "Yes." For this reason it is through him that we say the "Amen," to the glory of God.

We add our *"Amen"* to God's *"Yes."* God says *"Yes,"* and it's established in heaven. We say *"Amen"* to God's *"Yes"* and what's in heaven becomes established on earth. This is why Jesus taught us to declare:

Matthew 6:10 Your kingdom come. Your will be done, on earth as it is in heaven.

Jesus came as a man. He added a man's *"Amen"* to God's *"Yes,"* and heaven's reality was demonstrated on earth. Look at how Jesus' accomplished things by speaking. We would do well to follow his example!

Matthew 8:8, 13, 16 The centurion answered, "Lord, I am not worthy to have you come under my roof; but only speak the word, and my servant will be healed...And to the centurion Jesus said, "Go; let it be done for you according to your faith." And the servant was healed in that hour...That evening they brought to him many who were possessed with demons; and he cast out the spirits with a word, and cured all who were sick.

Remember Proverbs 11:11? *Through the blessing of the upright a city is exalted.* Here are some more scriptures which show the power of righteous declaration:

Proverbs 10:20 The tongue of the righteous is choice silver...

Proverbs 10:21 The lips of the righteous feed many...

Proverbs 12:18 Rash words are like sword thrusts, but the tongue of the wise brings healing.

Proverbs 15:4 (YLT) A healed tongue [is] a tree of life, And perverseness in it -- a breach in the spirit

Proverbs 18:20 From the fruit of the mouth one's stomach is satisfied; the yield of the lips brings satisfaction.

Proverbs 18:21 Death and life are in the power of the tongue

Praise and thanksgiving are a form of proclamation. When we praise and thank the Lord, we declare who he is. The heavenly reality that's in God's presence becomes established in this realm which the Lord has given to man, earth.

Psalm 22:3 Yet you are holy, enthroned on the praises of Israel.

What is praise but proclaiming who God is? We see God's nature in Jesus, and Jesus is called *"the Word."* When we praise the Lord, proclaiming his nature and goodness, we are proclaiming the word of the Lord with the authority that he's given us in the earth-realm.

John 1:1,14 In the beginning was the Word, and the Word was with God, and the Word was God... And the Word became flesh and lived among us, and we have seen his glory, the glory as of a father's only son, full of grace and truth.

God opens our eyes to see that his goodness fills the earth. As we thank him and proclaim his praise, we make the place we are become like heaven. We establish the dominion of his presence on this earth which he has given us.

A Sword In Your Mouth

Ephesians 6 presents us with the *"sword of the Spirit, which is the word of God."*[9] We read in Revelation of Jesus with a sword coming out of his mouth.[10] Psalms 149 also talks about using a sword as we sing God's praise.

---

[9] Ephesians 6:17
[10] Revelation 1:16. 19:15

Psalm 149:1-9 Praise the LORD! Sing to the LORD a new song, his praise in the assembly of the faithful. Let Israel be glad in its Maker; let the children of Zion rejoice in their King.

Let them praise his name with dancing, making melody to him with tambourine and lyre. For the LORD takes pleasure in his people; he adorns the humble with victory. Let the faithful exult in glory; let them sing for joy on their couches.

Let the high praises of God be in their throats and two-edged swords in their hands, to execute vengeance on the nations and punishment on the peoples, to bind their kings with fetters and their nobles with chains of iron, to execute on them the judgment decreed. This is glory for all his faithful ones. Praise the LORD!

I believe we can apply Psalm 149 today with a figurative understanding of the *"kings"* and *"nobles"* of the nations as the principalities and powers of darkness spoken of in Ephesians 6:12. They are the *"gods"* before whom we sing the Lord's praise: the spiritual forces of darkness behind violence, immorality, and every form of evil. They would like to capture our attention through fear.

When we declare God's praise, we execute vengeance on these powers which have blinded men's eyes from seeing the Lord's glory. We render them powerless. We are on the offence!

Constantly Proclaiming God's Praise

Scripture commands us to declare the Lord's praise. It speaks in several places of giving thanks and praise to God without ceasing. Here are some passages to consider:

Psalm 34:1-3, 5 I will bless the LORD at all times; his praise shall continually be in my mouth. My soul makes its boast in the LORD; let the humble hear and be glad. O magnify the LORD with me, and let us exalt his name together. Look to him, and be radiant; so your faces shall never be ashamed.

Psalm 35:28 Then my tongue shall tell of your righteousness and of your praise all day long.

Psalm 119:62 At midnight I rise to praise you…

Psalm 119:164 Seven times a day I praise you for your righteous ordinances.

When I first read these scriptures, I wondered how it was possible to constantly praise the Lord. I realized that to say, for example *"He's always talking about football,"* in English, doesn't mean that someone literally never stops talking about football. It does mean, however, he is pretty obsessed with it!

In the same way, we can think about the works of the Lord so much that our attention is fully captured by what the Holy Spirit is doing. Even when we aren't speaking, our hearts are constantly bursting with gratefulness to the Lord. We are impressed by God, in awe of him, and constantly aware of his presence.

That being said, I have experienced periods when I didn't stop thanking and praising God with my voice for a long time, until it felt like the very atmosphere around me was vibrating with the love of God. I continued to sing quietly even when I was with other people.

Praise Is Not Only Expressed Verbally

It's powerful when we use our mouths to declare God's goodness. Choosing our words carefully helps us to steer our thoughts and the rest of our being in the direction that we want them to go.

James 3:3-5 If we put bits into the mouths of horses to make them obey us, we guide their whole bodies. Or look at ships: though they are so large that it takes strong winds to drive them, yet they are guided by a very small rudder wherever the will of the pilot directs. So also the tongue is a small member, yet it boasts of great exploits.

When our minds and hearts are filled with praise and thanksgiving, all we do becomes a powerful proclamation of God's goodness. It changes our surroundings. We sing and speak God's praise verbally in order to direct our souls and entire beings to bless the Lord. King David spoke of his whole being, all that was within him, blessing the Lord.

Psalm 103:1-5 Bless the LORD, O my soul, and all that is within me, bless his holy name. Bless the LORD, O my soul, and do not forget all his benefits—who forgives all your iniquity, who heals all your diseases, who redeems your life from the Pit, who crowns you with steadfast love and mercy, who satisfies you with good as long as you live so that your youth is renewed like the eagle's.

Are all forms of communication expressed through intelligible language or even auditory means? Certainly not. Therefore it must be possible to declare God's praise by many means, even without words.

1 Thessalonians 5:18 (NASB) In everything give thanks; for this is God's will for you in Christ Jesus

Colossians 3:16-18 Let the word of Christ dwell in you richly; teach and admonish one another in all wisdom; and with gratitude in your hearts sing psalms, hymns, and spiritual songs to God. And whatever you do, in word or deed, do everything in the name of the Lord Jesus, giving thanks to God the Father through him.

Colossians 3:23 (NLT) Whatever work you do, do it with all your heart. Do it for the Lord and not for men.

It's interesting what we see when we look at a more literal interpretation of Colossians 3:23.

Colossians 3:23 (YLT) ...and all, whatever ye may do -- out of soul work -- as to the Lord, and not to men.

Colossians 3:23 (LEB) Whatever you do, accomplish it from the soul, as to the Lord, and not to people.

Psalm 103 speaks of the soul blessing the Lord. When our soul blesses the Lord, all we do becomes a proclamation of praise and thanksgiving to God.

Ephesians 5:18-20 Do not get drunk with wine, for that is debauchery; but be filled with the Spirit, as you sing psalms and hymns and spiritual songs among yourselves, singing and making melody to the Lord in your hearts, giving thanks to God the Father at all times and for everything in the name of our Lord Jesus Christ.

Notice how Ephesians says we can be continually filled with the Holy Spirit— singing to the Lord and giving thanks to God the Father at all times and for everything. In all that Jesus did and said, he revealed the nature of the heavenly Father to us, and he said the words he has given us are spirit and are life.[11] The proclamation of God's nature is spirit and life, and we are continuously filled with the Holy Spirit as we proclaim God's nature.

Those Who Look To You Are Radiant

Moses' face became radiant when he saw the glory of the Lord. Our faces can also radiate God's glory.

We direct our souls to bless the Lord by verbally declaring his praise and meditating on his works. When everything in us blesses the Lord, we become radiant. The light of God's glory emanates from our beings so that his presence can be tangibly felt wherever we go.

Our shining faces are a nonverbal proclamation. They cause the light of the knowledge of God's glory to dawn around us. When the light of the Lord's glory emanates from us, we witness miracles triggered by only a thought, before even a word is spoken. Further on, I will share a few testimonies of miracles that were caused by God-thoughts.

Remember this principle: when the eyes of your heart are opened to see the Lord's glory, God's light will shine through you so that those around you will see the Lord as well.

This is how you awaken the dawn. You choose to put your focus on God's goodness and glory. By declaring God's praise with your mouth, you direct your soul to bless the Lord. The eyes of your heart are opened to see the glory of the Lord; you become radiant; and your surroundings are filled with the light of the knowledge of the Lord's glory until they become like heaven.

I've met people who are radiant with the Lord's glory. They live as heavenly people. In *Present Access To Heaven* I mentioned the Christian camp I first

---

[11] John 6:63

attended when I was 10 years old. The people who ran that camp were radiant. Their lives emanated love and the joy of the Lord.

The camp's atmosphere was heavenly. God's love permeated everything. I was born again and set free on the way home when my mother spoke the words *"What is there to be depressed about?"* My eyes opened to see God's glory.

My experience around such people has put a passion in my heart to walk as a man of heaven as much as possible. I want my face to be glowing and my heart overflowing with the goodness of God. I want people to tangibly feel the Lord's presence when they are near me. I want their whole lives to change when I speak a few words.

Ps. 34:1-3, 5 I will bless the LORD at all times; his praise shall continually be in my mouth. My soul makes its boast in the LORD; let the humble hear and be glad. O magnify the LORD with me, and let us exalt his name together...Look to him, and be radiant; so your faces shall never be ashamed.

If I want my face to radiate God's glory, then I must look to him. How do I look to him? I proclaim his praise verbally until my whole soul is blessing the Lord. I discipline my thoughts to meditate on the mighty works of the Lord. I refuse to be impressed with any evil power or preoccupied with distracting things that steal my attention from the Lord's goodness! Read the story of Stephen:

Acts 4:8-15 Stephen, full of grace and power, did great wonders and signs among the people. Then some of those who belonged to the synagogue of the Freedmen (as it was called), Cyrenians, Alexandrians, and others of those from Cilicia and Asia, stood up and argued with Stephen. But they could not withstand the wisdom and the Spirit with which he spoke.

Then they secretly instigated some men to say, "We have heard him speak blasphemous words against Moses and God." They stirred up the people as well as the elders and the scribes; then they suddenly confronted him, seized him, and brought him before the council. They set up false witnesses who said, "This man never stops saying things against this holy place and the law; for we have heard him say that this Jesus of Nazareth will destroy this place and will change the customs that Moses handed on to us." And all who sat in the council looked intently at him, and they saw that his face was like the face of an angel.

Acts 7:54-60 When they heard these things, they became enraged and ground their teeth at Stephen. But filled with the Holy Spirit, he gazed into heaven and saw the glory of God and Jesus standing at the right hand of God. "Look," he said, "I see the heavens opened and the Son of Man standing at the right hand of God!"

But they covered their ears, and with a loud shout all rushed together against him. Then they dragged him out of the city and began to stone him; and the witnesses laid their coats at the feet of a young man named Saul. While they were stoning Stephen, he prayed, "Lord Jesus, receive my spirit." Then he knelt down and cried out in a loud voice, "Lord, do not hold this sin against them." When he had said this, he died.

All the hatred Stephen faced as he was on trial and stoned to death couldn't stop him from being filled with the Holy Spirit, looking into heaven, and beholding the glory of God. Even the hostile unbelievers saw that his face shone like that of an angel. Considering this, what circumstances can prevent me from looking into heaven and seeing the glory of the Lord until my face is radiant?

Acts says that Stephen was *"filled with the Holy Spirit."* I want to be filled with the Holy Spirit as Stephen was, so that my face shines with the light of God's glory. How do you think that he became so filled with the Holy Spirit? I have an idea.

Ephesians 5:18-20 Do not get drunk with wine, for that is debauchery; but be filled with the Spirit, as you sing psalms and hymns and spiritual songs among yourselves, singing and making melody to the Lord in your hearts, giving thanks to God the Father at all times and for everything in the name of our Lord Jesus Christ.

As the eyes of our hearts are opened we see the Lord as he is, we come to know the love of God that surpasses knowledge, and we are filled with all the fullness of God. The light of heaven emanates from our beings.

Psalm 89:14-17 Righteousness and justice are the foundation of your throne; steadfast love and faithfulness go before you. Happy are the people who know the festal shout, who walk, O LORD, in the light of your countenance; they exult in your name all day long, and extol your righteousness. For you are the glory of their strength; by your favor our horn is exalted.

How do we walk in the light of the Lord's countenance? By exalting in his name and extolling his righteousness all day long. When we do that, the light of his glory that we behold is reflected so that others can see it. We carry the knowledge of the glory of the Lord. Walk in God's light until you emit it.

In fact, one of the commonly used Hebrew words translated *"praise"* is *"halal."*[12] Part of the definition, according to Strong's concordance, is *"to shine"* or *"give light."* It is also to *"be clear,"* usually as in color.

In *Present Access to Heaven* I mentioned when whole families felt the weight of God's presence, sometimes with shivers going through their bodies. It's possible to be so full of the Lord's light that when you walk by people they tangibly feel the Lord's glory and are delivered from evil spirits.

Grammy's Vision

I remember when my grandmother (Grammy) had her first heavenly experience. She came from a traditional church background. Although she was open to much of the Holy Spirit's work, she didn't believe it when people talked about having visions of heaven.

Then one of her friends invited her to a Christian retreat with the Assemblies of God denomination. She listened to the speaker with interest and liked his message. At the end, her friend prodded her to go forward and receive prayer.

A long line of people were waiting for prayer, so she only joined them to make her friend happy. When the minister prayed for her, she fell on the grass and had a vision.

She saw Jesus come to her, shining with light. He had piercing eyes, full of such a love that she had no words to express it. Jesus took her to the Father.

God the Father was huge and so full of light that she couldn't see his face. It was too brilliant. But he took her like a little child onto his lap, and said *"I love you."*

Grammy lay on the grass for a long time while she was having this experience. When she came to her

---

[12] Strong's Hebrew And Greek Dictionaries, word H1984

senses, most of the people that had been around were gone. She was confused, in a state of shock, and asked everyone *"What happened to me?"* They had to explain it to her! Many of the people there believed in such encounters, but had never had one. Grammy hadn't believed in such experiences, yet she had one!

Before this she had undergone knee surgery which left lingering pain. Her knee was healed while she was having the vision.

Grammy told us about her vision a few days later, and we all rejoiced. There could be no doubt that she had seen the Lord. I had never seen her face so radiant, so full of light. Her very countenance was declaring God's praise! She looked 10 years younger. It's marvelous what seeing the Lord's glory will do to a person!

Even if we don't have a vision like Grammy did, we know from scripture that we can choose to behold God's glory. Our faces can become radiant with His light as well.

Turn your eyes upon Jesus,
Look full in his wonderful face[13]

Although I have never fallen on the ground and had a vision like Grammy did, I have also seen the Lord so that my being was filled with light. The eyes of my heart were opened as I sang praise and gave thanks to God. I experienced a love no words could express. As she was, I have also been physically healed as I beheld the glory of the Lord.

When our whole souls bless the Lord until we emanate his glory, all that we do becomes a proclamation of praise and thanksgiving to God. Like Psalm 19 describes, speech goes forth even without words.

---

[13] Hymn *Turn Your Eyes Upon Jesus* Helen H. Lemmel, 1922 Public Domain

Psalm 19:1-4 The heavens are telling the glory of God; and the firmament proclaims his handiwork. Day to day pours forth speech, and night to night declares knowledge. There is no speech, nor are there words; their voice is not heard; yet their voice goes out through all the earth, and their words to the end of the world.

The authority in the proclamation coming from your spirit as you bless the Lord will cause the light of the knowledge of God's glory to dawn all around you. I've experienced this to a small degree, but much more is possible.

In *Present Access To Heaven* I wrote how a little girl was healed when she saw me. I also mentioned the words of an elderly Russian lady, *"When I see you, it makes me want to live again."* What a thrill and privilege to shine the light of the Lord's glory! What scripture describes stirs up a hunger in my heart to walk in this reality more than I ever have before.

Acts 5:14-16 Yet more than ever believers were added to the Lord, great numbers of both men and women, so that they even carried out the sick into the streets, and laid them on cots and mats, in order that Peter's shadow might fall on some of them as he came by. A great number of people would also gather from the towns around Jerusalem, bringing the sick and those tormented by unclean spirits, and they were all cured.

People were healed when Peter came near them, because his soul blessed the Lord so that his very being gave thanks to God and proclaimed his praise. God's glory fills the whole earth, but it manifests tangibly when we declare it by giving thanks and praise to him.

Work

In *Present Access To Heaven* I described how I hated doing chores at home. Then when God touched my heart, the first thing I did was wash the dishes and sweep the floor.

Because my soul was blessing the Lord, washing the dishes and sweeping the floor became an expression of thanksgiving to God. They became a proclamation of the Lord's goodness. Although there were no words, the light of the Lord was shining as I worked.

When your heart is filled with thanksgiving towards God, you will express his love and joy through your work. You will become a heavenly person, shining with light. Blind eyes will be opened so that others will see the light of God's glory which fills the earth and fills your workplace. You will awaken the dawn.

Art, Colors, Banners, And Raising Hands

These are visual forms of communication. If we can use a medium to communicate, we can use it to proclaim God's goodness with authority. In fact, one of God's names in scripture, describing an aspect of his character, is *"The Lord my Banner."* (Jehovah-Nissi)

Exodus 17:9-15 Moses said to Joshua, "Choose some men for us and go out, fight with Amalek. Tomorrow I will stand on the top of the hill with the staff of God in my hand." So Joshua did as Moses told him, and fought with Amalek, while Moses, Aaron, and Hur went up to the top of the hill. Whenever Moses held up his hand, Israel prevailed; and whenever he lowered his hand, Amalek prevailed.

But Moses' hands grew weary; so they took a stone and put it under him, and he sat on it. Aaron and Hur held up his hands, one on one side, and the other on the other side; so his hands were steady until the sun set. And Joshua defeated Amalek and his people with the sword. And Moses built an altar and called it, The Lord is my banner. He said, "A hand upon the banner of the Lord!

This story shows the connection between raising our hands, and the name *"The Lord my Banner."* It also shows us that saying *"The Lord is my Banner"* is like saying *"The Lord is my Victory."* When we raise our hands to glorify the Lord we proclaim one of God's names, an aspect of his nature. We declare that he is our victory.

1 Timothy 2:8 I desire, then, that in every place the men should pray, lifting up holy hands without anger or argument.

I remember feeling a desire to raise my hands to the Lord, but I was embarrassed to do so. When I finally did, they started to vibrate with God's glory and I began to weep. I felt his presence like a weight around me. As I declared God's glory by raising my hands, I began to experience it.

In the Old Testament, we read that God anointed a man named *"Bezalel"* with artistic ability.

Exodus 31:1-5 The LORD spoke to Moses: See, I have called by name Bezalel son of Uri son of Hur, of the tribe of Judah: and I have filled him with divine spirit, with ability, intelligence, and knowledge in every kind of craft, to devise artistic designs, to work in gold, silver, and bronze, in cutting stones for setting, and in carving wood, in every kind of craft.

The name *"Bezalel"* means *"In God's shadow."*[14] Consider the account in the book of Acts of people healed and delivered as they came under Peter's shadow. Peter was so full of the God's presence that the Lord's shadow became his shadow.

Bezalel was of the tribe of Judah, meaning *"praise."*[15] He declared God's praise through his artistic abilities. He created art which testified of God's nature and pointed to heavenly realities. His art proclaimed the glory of God to those who entered the Jewish tabernacle.

F.F. Bosworth, in his book *Christ The Healer*[16], talks about *"seven redemptive names"* of God found in scripture. Since reading *Christ The Healer*, I've learned that the Bible scholar C.I. Scofield also wrote about these. Each of these names communicates a redemptive facet of God's nature. Here they are.

Jehovah-Shalom—The Lord is our Peace
Jehovah-Raha—The Lord is my Shepherd
Jehovah-Jirah—The Lord will provide
Jehovah-Nissi—The Lord our Banner or Victor
Jehovah-Tsidkenu—The Lord our Righteousness
Jehovah-Rapha—The Lord our Healer
Jehovah-Shammah—The Lord is present

After reading these seven *"redemptive names,"* I thought it interesting that scripture says God is light, and a rainbow is composed of light refracted into seven colors. Scripture talks about the seven spirits of the Lord.

---

[14] Strong's Hebrew and Greek Dictionaries, word H1212
[15] Strong's Hebrew and Greek Dictionaries, words H3063 and H3034
[16] Bosworth, F.F. *Christ the Healer*, Page 90-91. Grand Rapids: Chosen Books, 2008

1 John 1:5 This is the message we have heard from him and proclaim to you, that God is light and in him there is no darkness at all.

Revelation 21:23 And the city has no need of sun or moon to shine on it, for the glory of God is its light, and its lamp is the Lamb.

Revelation 4:5 ... in front of the throne burn seven flaming torches, which are the seven spirits of God

Revelation 5:6 Then I saw between the throne and the four living creatures and among the elders a Lamb standing as if it had been slaughtered, having seven horns and seven eyes, which are the seven spirits of God sent out into all the earth.

Could it be that each color of the rainbow represents a facet of God's nature and could even correspond to one of the redemptive names of the Lord? We do know that different colors evoke different responses and feelings. I've even theorized about which of the seven colors of the rainbow could correspond to each of the seven redemptive names that Bosworth wrote about.

I surely wouldn't teach this as a scripturally provable doctrine, but it is an intriguing idea. What is clear to me, however, is that we can use colors, banners, and other visual means to praise the Lord and declare his glory with power and authority, so that what is real in heaven becomes real in our realm, earth. Expression through these arts is potent when it comes from a soul that is blessing the Lord.

Dancing, Spinning, Rejoicing

One of the words translated *"rejoice," "be glad,"* or *"joy"* in the Old Testament literally means *"to spin."* It makes us think of little children spinning with glee. Spinning is a natural expression of joy. Look at Strong's definition of this word, "gîyl" [17]

A primitive root; properly to spin around (under the influence of any violent emotion), that is, usually rejoice, or (as cringing) fear: - be glad, joy, be joyful, rejoice.

When I shared my experiences in Russia and Belize I mentioned becoming aware of everything around me, even the buildings, proclaiming God's glory. Scripture describes the earth itself rejoicing in the Lord as it spins. The earth is spinning in praise!

1 Chronicles 16:31 Let the heavens be glad, and let the earth rejoice, and let them say among the nations, "The LORD is king!

Psalm 96:11 Let the heavens be glad, and let the earth rejoice; let the sea roar, and all that fills it

Psalm 97:1 The LORD is king! Let the earth rejoice; let the many coastlands be glad!

As people spin and dance, rejoicing in the Lord, they are proclaiming his glory. This proclamation has authority because it was to mankind that God gave dominion over creation.

Here are a few of the many scriptural references to people rejoicing, using this word meaning literally *"to spin."* Notice the scriptures that refer to rejoicing in God's salvation, and rejoicing in his deliverance.

---

[17] Strong's Hebrew And Greek Dictionaries, word H1523

Psalm 9:14 ...I may recount all your praises, and, in the gates of daughter Zion, rejoice in your deliverance.

Psalm 32:11 Be glad in the LORD and rejoice, O righteous, and shout for joy, all you upright in heart.

Psalm 89:16 (KJV) In thy name shall they rejoice all the day: and in thy righteousness shall they be exalted.

Isaiah 25:9 ...This is the LORD for whom we have waited; let us be glad and rejoice in his salvation.

Isaiah 61:10 I will greatly rejoice in the LORD, my whole being shall exult in my God; for he has clothed me with the garments of salvation, he has covered me with the robe of righteousness

When we spin for joy because of God's deliverance and salvation, we are proclaiming salvation! We are releasing the word of the Lord. It is not a verbal proclamation, but we can still see miraculous results. Thank you for saving me, Jesus!

Scripture even uses this word meaning *"to spin"* to describe the Lord himself rejoicing over his people. What love the Lord has for us!

Zephaniah 3:17 The LORD, your God, is in your midst, a warrior who gives victory; he will rejoice over you with gladness, he will renew you in his love; he will exult over you with loud singing

There are many other physical expressions of praise and thanksgiving to God. Scripture exhorts us to praise the Lord with our bodies.

Psalm 150:4 Praise him with tambourine and dance; praise him with strings and pipe!

I myself am a pretty clumsy dancer. When I was young, growing up in a charismatic church, I felt self-conscious and embarrassed to dance in worship with everyone else.

I don't mention these various expressions of praise to tell anyone how to express your thanks to God! Yet I am pointing out the value of many different forms of heartfelt expression. If your heart moves you to do something out of thanksgiving to God, why not try it?

Even though I may not dance in the same way some people do, I've come to enjoy physically expressing my thanks to the Lord. I often move in some way when we sing praise, even if it's a bit awkward. I had a wonderful time in Russia holding hands with the old ladies and dancing in circles with them, singing praise to God! That didn't take so much coordination. I also jump with joy after I see God heal people.

There's something special about using our bodies to express thanks to the Lord. We give ourselves completely to the Lord—body, soul, and spirit. When I've expressed praise through movement, I've sometimes been overwhelmed with the awareness of my whole body belonging to the Lord. That awareness often came with a tangible feeling of the Holy Spirit's power flowing through my physical body.

The body is sacred and holy to the Lord. The Lord is the savior of the body.[18] It is significantly powerful when we use our bodies to magnify the Lord. It's a special honor to know that our bodies belong to him, and to be able to feel his presence in our bodies.

---

[18] Ephesians 5:23

Playing, Bubbles, And Other Forms Of Expression

I love children. As a teenager and young adult, I spent much time volunteering with children. They are such a gift from God; so funny and delightful! I've often felt my soul bursting with thankfulness to God for the children.

Young children love bubbles! I took a bottle of bubble soap with me on many mission trips. The kids ran around with delight, chasing the bubbles and trying to pop them.

To me, bubbles have come to symbolize joy and delight. Are these not aspects of God's nature, heavenly realities?

Psalm 16:11 You show me the path of life. In your presence there is fullness of joy; in your right hand are pleasures forevermore.

Psalm 37:4 Take delight in the LORD, *and he will give you the desires of your heart.*

Psalm 36:8 They feast on the abundance of your house, and you give them drink from the river of your delights.

Relationship with the Lord is a mutual delight. The Lord also delights in us!

2 Samuel 22:20 He brought me out into a broad place; he delivered me, because he delighted in me.

Psalm 16:3 As for the holy ones in the land, they are the noble, in whom is all my delight.

Psalm 147:10-11 His delight is not in the strength of the horse, nor his pleasure in the speed of a runner; but the

LORD *takes pleasure in those who fear him, in those who hope in his steadfast love.*

Though I was playing with the kids when I blew bubbles, I soon began to do this with the intention of declaring the glory of God and heavenly reality. As I blew bubbles at the kids, in my heart I released the Lord's blessing on their lives. I also released heavenly reality to the country or city I was visiting. My heart was screaming *"This country is full of God's glory, and may every person know the joy and delight that come from knowing him."*

One of the first times I preached in a church on a Sunday morning, I brought bubble soap. I talked about the joy of the Lord and becoming like little children. And I blew bubbles at the people!

Many Christians who've discovered their authority in Christ to heal the sick find that they can do strange things, with intention, and people are healed. They point at the sick person, stand beside them, or give them an apple, and the pain leaves!

What's happening is that the believer's soul is blessing the Lord, declaring that he is the Healer and thanking him. Their being has become radiant, whether it is visible with the naked eye or not, and light is going out as a proclamation. This is praise, because it's a declaration of an aspect of God's nature.

When our souls bless the Lord, we can do many things with intention, whether blowing bubbles or something else, and the action becomes a declaration which brings people into an experiential knowledge of the Lord's glory. That may manifest as healing, deliverance, joy, peace, or a heart that is suddenly changed.

But remember, it's with the verbal proclamation of praise and thanksgiving that we direct our souls to bless the Lord. As our souls bless they Lord, they become so full of light that anything we do from a heart of thanksgiving to God becomes a powerful proclamation of the Lord's glory, awakening the dawn!

5. Drawing Water From The Wells Of Salvation

Isaiah 12

Isaiah chapter 12 gives us the picture of drawing water from the wells of salvation. What are the wells of salvation, and how do we draw water from them? First let's read the passage:

Isaiah 12:2-6 Surely God is my salvation; I will trust, and will not be afraid, for the Lord God is my strength and my might; he has become my salvation.

With joy you will draw water from the wells of salvation. And you will say in that day: Give thanks to the Lord, call on his name; make known his deeds among the nations; proclaim that his name is exalted.

Sing praises to the Lord, for he has done gloriously; let this be known in all the earth. Shout aloud and sing for joy, O royal Zion, for great in your midst is the Holy One of Israel.

Thanking God For His Deliverance

In *Present Access To Heaven,* we discussed past, present, and future salvation. This series focuses on salvation in the present, which is God's continuing deliverance.

My personal experience and other passages of scripture lead me to this conclusion about Isaiah 12: each instance of God's deliverance in the past is a well of salvation. Each story of God's work holds a revelation of

God's nature and a deposit of his power. We draw water from the wells of salvation when we proclaim and give thanks for what God has done before.

In the *Proclamation* chapter, we explored how God accomplishes his will through his word. When we tell stories about what God has done, we are also proclaiming the word of God. We aren't just proclaiming God's works, but his nature, as it is revealed through his works. By doing so, we are again saying *"amen"* to God's *"yes"*—— proclaiming the word of the Lord so that the same thing happens again.

Every story of God's deliverance is precious to me. I love to ask other believers how they came to know the Lord, and what God has done in their lives. The stories I've heard amaze me! I also continue to remind myself what God has done in my life. I have found that when I can't stop talking about God's deliverance, the same miracles happen again! Here are some of my experiences which demonstrate this.

Laying Hands On The Blind Lady

My brother and I met a blind lady after the evening session of a Christian conference. We started talking with her and her friends. When we realized she was blind, we asked if we could lay our hands on her eyes. She welcomed healing ministry.

We first interviewed her about the condition. She was legally blind and could not see color. She could see light and darkness, but not much more. Then we laid our hands on her and began to command her eyes to see.

She felt a current like electricity flowing in her eyes, and we felt heat as a manifestation of God's power. This was exciting, and we continued on for some time. She did begin to see some color and reported slight improvement in her vision. However, after quite a while, her vision was still terrible. I think she still would have been evaluated as legally blind by a doctor.

I had been laying my hands on many people, seeing many miracles, and constantly talking about all that God did and rejoicing in His goodness. However, I always tried to share stories with as much accuracy and integrity as possible. Talking about God's mighty works is simply good stewardship. We have a responsibility to share God's deliverance with others.

So the next Wednesday, I shared this as a testimony at the youth meeting. I didn't exaggerate, but I thanked God that as we laid hands on her, she felt his power and had some slight improvement. I shared that she still had a long way to go, but I knew that God wants us to open the eyes of the blind like Jesus did, and that we are growing in God's power and grace, so I was excited to see such a manifestation when laying hands on a blind lady.

This shows something about walking in faith. I wasn't focusing on what didn't happen. I was rejoicing in what the Lord did and was doing. I wasn't going to let that which didn't happen steal my joy and gratitude to God for what did happen. I was beholding the goodness of the Lord and refusing to let anything else take my attention from him.

Vision Instantly Restored

As I was sharing this testimony —— not of a blind lady being fully healed, but of a blind lady feeling God's power and having slight improvement —— my sister Christina blurted out *"I feel something moving in my eyes."*

I was drawing water from a well of salvation as I thanked God for what he was doing with the blind lady, and so releasing the word of God. It triggered something supernatural, again. I found out that if I would talk all

57

day long about God's miracles and deliverance, miracles would happen all around me.

That weekend my sister went to the eye doctor. He was surprised and said *"I don't usually say this, but I recommend that you stop wearing your glasses."* My sister had been almost instantly healed of farsightedness, unexpectedly, as I was thanking God that the blind lady felt his power. Heaven now!

Similar miracles have happened many times. We talk about what God has done, and the same thing happens again. Contained within each testimony of God's salvation, is a deposit of the power of God, a well. When we tell the stories and thank God for what he did before, we are declaring God's word and the same power is put into play in the present.

The Crippled Lady And Her Husband

Once someone told me a testimony from their family. There was a married couple, and the wife was a Christian, but was crippled and in a wheelchair. The husband was a rough guy with a bad character. His wife prayed for many years for him to come to the Lord, but he was hardened.

One day, after all those years, he opened his heart after hearing someone preach, and responded that he wanted to give his life to Jesus. When his wife saw him walking down the aisle of that church, she was shocked! She jumped up, forgetting that she was in a wheelchair, and never used it again.

When I heard this story, even though it was from many decades ago, I was overwhelmed by the joy of salvation and felt a wave of God's power course through my body. I felt the same power of God that caused this to happen many decades ago, suddenly released in the present as I heard the story. The same grace and power of God that brought deliverance in the past, are released again when we praise and thank the Lord for what he has done.

Declaring The Works Of The Lord

Praise isn't only singing. It's also telling people in your conversations about what the Lord has done. I've met many Christians who have remarkable stories of how they came to know Christ and how God has delivered them, but I rarely hear such stories unless I ask. This shouldn't be so. I believe we have a responsibility to tell others about what the Lord has done.

Read Psalm 71 and determine in your heart that like David, your mouth with be filled with the Lord's praise and with his glory all day long. Decide that you will proclaim the Lord's mighty works. As you do so, you will begin to walk in heaven while on earth. Manifestations of the Lord's glory and deliverance will spring up all around you.

Psalm 71:6-8, 14-18 Upon you I have leaned from my birth; it was you who took me from my mother's womb. My praise is continually of you. I have been like a portent to many, but you are my strong refuge. My mouth is filled with your praise, and with your glory all day long....

But I will hope continually, and will praise you yet more and more. My mouth will tell of your righteous acts, of your deeds of salvation all day long, though their number is past my knowledge. I will come praising the mighty deeds of the Lord GOD, I will praise your righteousness, yours alone. O God, from my youth you have taught me, and I still proclaim your wondrous deeds. So even to old age and gray hairs, O God, do not forsake me, until I proclaim your might to all the generations to come. Your power and your righteousness, O God, reach the high heavens....

I will also praise you with the harp for your faithfulness, O my God; I will sing praises to you with the lyre, O Holy One of Israel. My lips will shout for joy when I sing praises to you; my soul also, which you have rescued. All day long my tongue will talk of your righteous help...

I first began to experience miracles through my hands after being in a place where I saw many miracles happen. I didn't feel like I had much faith. However, what I saw the Lord do impacted me so much, that I began to talk about it all the time. I became obsessed with the works of the Lord.

I began spending up to three hours at a time reading testimonies and watching videos of what the Holy Spirit was doing. It's natural to talk the most about what we are thinking. The first step in learning to constantly praise the Lord is to meditate on what he has done. Study the works of the Lord. Delight in them. Meditate on the majesty of the Lord and on what he has done. Look at the following passages from Psalms.

Psalm 111:1-4 Praise the LORD! I will give thanks to the LORD with my whole heart, in the company of the upright, in the congregation. Great are the works of the LORD, studied by all who delight in them. Full of honor and majesty is his work, and his righteousness endures forever. He has gained renown by his wonderful deeds; the LORD is gracious and merciful.

Psalm 145 I will extol you, my God and King, and bless your name forever and ever. Every day I will bless you, and praise your name forever and ever. Great is the LORD, and greatly to be praised; his greatness is unsearchable.

One generation shall laud your works to another, and shall declare your mighty acts. On the glorious splendor of your majesty, and on your wondrous works, I will meditate.

The might of your awesome deeds shall be proclaimed, and I will declare your greatness. They shall celebrate the fame of your abundant goodness, and shall sing aloud of your righteousness.

The LORD is gracious and merciful, slow to anger and abounding in steadfast love. The LORD is good to all, and his compassion is over all that he has made.

All your works shall give thanks to you, O LORD, and all your faithful shall bless you. They shall speak of the glory of your kingdom, and tell of your power, to make known to all people your mighty deeds, and the glorious splendor of your kingdom. Your kingdom is an everlasting kingdom, and your dominion endures throughout all generations.

It's easy to forget the wonderful things the Lord has done for us. Facebook has a feature which shows us what we posted on the same day several years ago. Just today, I read a Facebook post from three years ago. It said *"That lady I posted about the other day— her surgery was cancelled today. Thank you Jesus!"*

I saw this post today, and I don't even remember who the woman was or what the problem was! But I was glad that Facebook reminded me of another surgery that was cancelled because of the goodness of God touching someone's body.

It's worth making a journal or log of what you have seen the Holy Spirit do; of his deliverance in your life and the lives of those around you. I often wish I had recorded more of what the Lord has done. So many miracles have happened that I forget many of them unless I'm reminded — either by reading something I wrote or by talking with someone who reminds me of the time I prayed and God healed them.

Shouts Of Deliverance

As I teenager, I found myself shouting with joy because of what the Lord had done for me. When I was 18 and went to Belize, my attention was drawn to the scriptures speaking of shouts of joy and salvation.

The Holy Spirit highlighted Psalm 32:7 for me. I wanted to be surrounded with shouts of salvation as the Lord delivered people wherever I went. I took this scripture as a promise and continued to speak and meditate on it.

Psalm 32:7 (ESV) You are a hiding place for me; you preserve me from trouble; you surround me with shouts of deliverance. Selah

Psalm 32:7 (GW) You are my hiding place. You protect me from trouble. You surround me with joyous songs of salvation

Some translations talk about *"shouts of deliverance,"* and some translate this verse *"songs of salvation,"* *"victory,"* or something else. I like to think of it as *"shouts of salvation."*

I realized that by shouting with joy and thanksgiving because the Lord saved me, I was proclaiming salvation. Something was happening in the spiritual realm. The word of the Lord was being released, so that the deliverance I experienced would happen for others.

Scripture also refers to *"shouts of joy."* I realized that the *"shouts of deliverance"* in scripture are the same as the *"shouts of joy."* The shouts of joy are shouts of salvation, because they spring from the joy of salvation.

Experiencing God's deliverance and salvation produces tremendous joy.

Psalm 51:12 Restore to me the joy of your salvation.

Isaiah 12:3 With joy you will draw water from the wells of salvation.

Here are some scriptures I began to meditate on, that talk about shouts of joy. :

Job 8:21 He will yet fill your mouth with laughter, and your lips with shouts of joy.

Psalm 27:6 Now my head is lifted up above my enemies all around me, and I will offer in his tent sacrifices with shouts of joy; I will sing and make melody to the Lord.

Psalm 126:1-6 When the Lord restored the fortunes of Zion, we were like those who dream. Then our mouth was filled with laughter, and our tongue with shouts of joy; then it was said among the nations, "The Lord has done great things for them." The Lord has done great things for us, and we rejoiced.

Restore our fortunes, O Lord, like the watercourses in the Negeb. May those who sow in tears reap with shouts of joy. Those who go out weeping, bearing the seed for sowing, shall come home with shouts of joy, carrying their sheaves.

I remember hearing a lady give testimony of all the Lord had delivered her from. She had an ugly past, full of drug abuse, prostitution, and oppression by the devil. After sharing all the Lord had done in her life, she doubled over and shouted with all her strength *"Ho!"* She was radiant.

It was a shout that came from the very depths of her being. I think it lasted almost 30 seconds. As she shouted, I felt the power of the Lord being released to save people and deliver them from addiction and oppression. This shout was a proclamation *"Do it again, God!"*

Remember my experience in Belize? When my eyes were opened to see the glory of the Lord filling Orange Walk, I began to shout. My heart was exploding with the joy of salvation and with thankfulness for what the Lord had done for me. Soon after that happening, many young people experienced the Lord's deliverance, just as I had.

Laughter

We just read a few verses that mentioned laughter. When my eyes were opened to see the Lord, everything the devil had done looked so small, weak, and unimpressive to me. I couldn't stop laughing! I became so impressed with the Lord that the things which used to seem big to me, now looked small in comparison.

Several times, I've started laughing when faced with a sickness that someone had. I was laughing because my mind was so filled with the works of the Lord that my reaction was *"another person is about to be healed!"* I wasn't laughing in unbelief, like Sarah did, but in faith!

In my book, *The Power-And-Love Sandwich*, I tell the story of my great-aunt. Her crooked back straightened as I laughed and spoke to it. On another occasion, an 86-year old woman was healed of several serious life-threatening conditions. I laughed as I prayed for her.

One of the most beautiful sounds I've ever heard was the sound of weeping and wailing turning to laughter. The weeping and wailing was the sound of people realizing their need for salvation and turning to the Lord. The laughter was the joy of salvation. The people began to laugh hysterically as they realized they had been forgiven and accepted by Father God.

Clapping

In the last chapter we talked about spinning for joy. This also can be a proclamation of salvation. Another non-verbal form of proclamation that we see in scripture is clapping. Again we see even creation itself, full of the glory of God, praising the Lord!

Isaiah 55:12 For you shall go out in joy, and be led back in peace; the mountains and the hills before you shall burst into song, and all the trees of the field shall clap their hands.

What is exciting in this verse is that the creation itself responds with praise to God as we rejoice in the Lord. This verse has meant much to me on my mission trips. When I go somewhere, I expect the mountains and hills to burst into song before me and the trees themselves to rejoice.

The following verses show clapping as a declaration of the dominion and righteous judgment of the Lord. He is a great King over all the earth!

Psalm 98:8-9 Let the floods clap their hands; let the hills sing together for joy at the presence of the LORD, for he is coming to judge the earth. He will judge the world with righteousness, and the peoples with equity.

Psalm 47:1 Clap your hands, all you peoples; shout to God with loud songs of joy. For the LORD, the Most High, is awesome, a great king over all the earth.

When we praise God with clapping, we should understand that we're proclaiming the kingdom of heaven is at hand. We're declaring God's kingship. By our words and proclamation we exercise the dominion of heaven, and we see heaven manifest wherever we go. God's grace will super-abound where sin has abounded, bringing heaven's dominion and undoing the works of the devil.

Heaven is here now
He's all around us
Heaven is Jesus[19]

---

[19] *Heaven Is Here*, Jesus Culture Music 2009

6. How Angels Become Active

He Rides On The Wings Of The Wind

Sometimes when a person is healed or another miracle happens, people ask *"Was that the Holy Spirit, or an angel?"* The answer is often *"both."* It was the Lord's presence as carried by an angel. Look at Psalm 18.

Psalm 18:6, 10 In my distress I called upon the LORD; to my God I cried for help. From his temple he heard my voice, and my cry to him reached his ears...He rode on a cherub, and flew; he came swiftly upon the wings of the wind.

Wait a second. A cherub is a kind of winged angel. They are often mentioned in scripture, along with descriptions of God's manifest glory. So God rides on angels?

God placed cherubim (plural) in the Garden of Eden when Adam and Eve left.[20] There were gold cherubim on both sides of the Ark of the Covenant[21] and woven in to the design of the temple.[22] God spoke to Moses from between the cherubim.[23] In several places, scripture describes God being enthroned on or between the cherubim.[24] Ezekiel said that the sound of the cherubim's wings sounded like the voice of God.

---

[20] Genesis 3:24
[21] Exodus 25:19-20
[22] Exodus 26:1
[23] Numbers 7:89
[24] 1 Chronicles 13:6, Psalm 99:1 and many others

Ezekiel 10:5 The sound of the wings of the cherubim was heard as far as the outer court, like the voice of God Almighty when he speaks.

Psalm 104 gives us further insight into how God could *"ride"* on an angel. In both Hebrew and Greek, the primary words translated *"angel"* also mean *"messenger."* This is because angels are messengers. They carry God's word.

Psalm 104:1-4 (NIV) Praise the L<small>ORD</small>*, my soul.* L<small>ORD</small> *my God, you are very great; you are clothed with splendor and majesty. The* L<small>ORD</small> *wraps himself in light as with a garment; he stretches out the heavens like a tent and lays the beams of his upper chambers on their waters.*

He makes the clouds his chariot and rides on the wings of the wind. He makes winds his messengers, flames of fire his servants.

First we read the description of the Lord's glory in Psalm 104, including being wrapped with light and coming on a cloud. This description corresponds with several other passages of scripture. Then we read again about God riding —— on the wings of the wind.

The word *"wind"* here is most often translated *"spirit."* It's the same word, and several translations translate it as *"spirits"* in verse 4. In the same way, the word *"messengers"* is the same word as *"angels,"* in both Hebrew and Greek. The NIV translation confirms this with a footnote after the word *"messengers,"* saying *"or angels."* Some translations do translate this word in verse 4 as *"angels."*

Psalm 104:4 (GW) You make your angels winds and your servants flames of fire.

Angels are ministering spirits, or winds. They are messengers because they carry God's word and proclaim it. God rides on them in the sense that they carry his presence by carrying his word. When Angels proclaim what the Lord is saying, God's presence manifests.

John 1:1,14 In the beginning was the Word, and the Word was with God, and the Word was God... And the Word became flesh and lived among us, and we have seen his glory, the glory as of a father's only son, full of grace and truth.

Angels proclaim God's word, just like we are called to proclaim God's word. By carrying God's word, they carry God's manifest presence. This is how God *"rides"* on them. As we proclaim the gospel, we also release the power of God. God has sent angels to help and serve us.

Hebrews 1:14 (NIV) Are not all angels ministering spirits sent to serve those who will inherit salvation?

Why Angels?

Some people ask *"Why do we need to talk about angels?"* They're concerned talking about angels will lead to an unhealthy obsession, or even angel worship.

The answer is simple. God has chosen to use angels. God could have done everything himself, but he chose to have men partner with him in his work. In the same way, God has chosen to have angels partner with him in accomplishing his will. For both men and angels, this is an honor and a privilege.

Of course we shouldn't worship angels! They are servants of the Lord, as we are. The apostle John encountered an angel carrying so much of the Lord's glory he was tempted to worship it. The angel told John he was only a fellow servant with him.

Revelation 19:9-10 And the angel said to me, "Write this: Blessed are those who are invited to the marriage supper of the Lamb." And he said to me, "These are true words of God." Then I fell down at his feet to worship him, but he said to me, "You must not do that! I am a fellow servant with you and your comrades who hold the testimony of Jesus. Worship God! For the testimony of Jesus is the spirit of prophecy."

We worship God! But we do thank him for angels. Angels are gifts from God, sent to help us, and so it's right to thank the Lord for them. It's also right to honor them, not at all as worship, but in the same way we honor a brother or sister in Christ who has something from the Lord to minister to us. We recognize that angels carry God's grace. The Lord himself has chosen to honor them by giving them the privilege of carrying his presence.

I think people often miss out on something the Lord has for them because they are afraid of angels. If the Lord has chosen to minister his grace by means of angels, then we should receive his messengers.

What Activates Angels?

I've experienced angelic activity many times, and I've noticed what seems to trigger that activity. My experience is in line with the testimony of scripture. Angels respond to God's word.

Psalm 103:20-21 Bless the LORD, O you his angels, you mighty ones who do his bidding, obedient to his spoken word. Bless the LORD, all his hosts, his ministers that do his will.

It's important to note that angels are not the ones God put in charge of this earth. God gave authority to human beings! Angels are sent to help and minister to us!

Hebrews 2:5-8 Now God did not subject the coming world, about which we are speaking, to angels. But someone has testified somewhere, "What are human beings that you are mindful of them, or mortals, that you care for them? You have made them for a little while lower than the angels; you have crowned them with glory and honor, subjecting all things under their feet."

Angels are eager to minister and to respond to the word of the Lord. However, because God has given authority on earth to mankind, they eagerly wait for a person to speak God's word. Angels wait for us because God didn't give dominion over the earth to them, but to us.

Therefore, they partner with us and with the Holy Spirit, all working together. They wait for us to do or say something to give them the go-ahead. God didn't have to involve men and angels in his work. Scripture teaches he's chosen to work in this way because he loves us and wants relationship with us. He wants us to share in his glory.[25] Both men and angels have the privilege of carrying God's presence.

Winds

We quoted the scripture *"He makes his angels winds…"* I've often felt the presence of angels as winds which carried a sense of God's presence.

This is common in times of singing praise to the Lord. Angels love to praise God! As we sing praise and give thanks to God, we're proclaiming his goodness and

---

[25] Romans 8:17, John 17:22

nature. We're essentially proclaiming the word of the Lord. Angels respond to this and minister the presence of God that we're singing of. When this happens people feel God's peace and joy, are spontaneously healed, or encounter God in other supernatural ways.

When sharing testimonies is combined with with singing and dancing to the Lord, the place becomes filled with many angels. I've sensed these angels as gusts of wind going around the room, and have heard the testimonies of people who have seen them.

In my 20's I owned and lived in two different houses in the United States which I shared with housemates. In both of these houses, I had a place where I wrote scriptures and prayers on the walls and ceilings. As I gave thanks to God, I was inspired to declare God's word in written form.

My housemates told me of experiences they had. Once I was gone for a few weeks, and came back to hear they thought there was an angel on the porch. Everyone who drove by stared at the same place on the porch, as if they were seeing something. One friend said *"Some really weird things are happening in your house. They're weird, but good."*

Another friend had begun to regularly see angels. She saw them in both my houses, and she told me there was one that always stood at the bottom of my stairs. I couldn't see this angel, but I could feel something as I walked through that area, like a vibration in the air.

At the time, I was a roofer and also installed replacement windows. I had put replacement windows in my whole house, and insulated them well. On Wednesday nights, I volunteered with our church's youth group.

One week, we worked in another state. It was a long drive, so I had to get up early. After youth group, two brothers asked me if they could stop by my house to talk before I dropped them off at their place.

They wanted my advice. I was really tired, but I thought, *"OK, we'll stop by my house, we'll talk for a while, and then I'll take them home.*

We talked about the issue. When we were done, I asked them if they'd ever received Holy Spirit baptism. They said *"No,"* so I prayed for them to be baptized in the Holy Spirit.

The younger of the two brothers started speaking in tongues and got very excited. He began to pray for everything imaginable. I remember his praying *"God, make my aunt's hair grow back..."* I was tired, and it was late. I thought, *"OK, he's excited. I'll let him pray until he calms down a little bit, and then I'll take everyone home. It's getting really late."*

Then something happened. Every few seconds, a gush of wind hit me. I felt winds going in circles around the room. Every time one of these gushes of wind hit me, I felt God's peace in the wind.

I'm fairly pragmatic, so when I experience something like this, I consider if there could be any natural explanation. But there wasn't. It wasn't windy outside. Even if it were windy, I had well-insulated, newly installed replacement windows. No heating or cooling system was running in my house, and the winds were going in circles!

As tired as I was, I didn't want to go to bed when the Holy Spirit was doing something! I ended up staying there for quite a bit longer. I didn't take the guys home until the winds stopped. By the time I got to bed, it was about 3:00 A.M. I got about two hours of sleep that night!

What triggered this experience? The angels began going in circles around my room as this young guy got excited about the Lord and began to pray and declare redemption with thanksgiving towards God.

Angels And Drawing Water From The Wells Of Salvation

The subject of angelic activity closely ties in with drawing water from the wells of salvation. When we proclaim something God has done in the past, angels take that as the word of the Lord on which to act. When we rejoice in what God has done, angels take that as the *"go ahead"* from men, who have been given dominion in this earth-realm. I've seen this play out in experience many times.

When my sister's eyes were healed (as she heard the testimony of a blind lady's healing) was it the Holy Spirit or an angel at work? I'm sure it was both. Just talking about eyes being healed and rejoicing in the Lord, was enough for that angel to act. The angel was carrying the presence of God, which was what made my sister's eyes adjust.

Verbal proclamation is not always necessary. I've had some interesting encounters with angelic activity while watching the Holy Spirit move on You Tube videos. Those experiences have impressed me with how real the spirit realm is.

It seems everything in the spirit realm works through proclamation. Angels proclaim God's goodness and his word, while fallen angels proclaim lies to try to blind people and keep them from seeing the glory of the Lord which fills the earth.

Once I was sitting downstairs in my parent's house, watching videos on You Tube of people ministering healing. I was intentionally filling my mind with what the Holy Spirit was doing, and rejoicing in it.

My sister walked by, coming from the kitchen, as I was watching a video of some young people laying hands on a person whose head needed to be healed. In the video, all the young people were whooping and hollering and thanking God for what he was doing.

I had a headset on. My sister had no idea what I was watching. She couldn't hear it. She didn't see it either, because she came from behind the computer. But when she passed me, she suddenly felt a heat come over her head. She remarked, *"Hey, my head just got really hot when I walked by you."*

My sister had been suffering from a concussion. I wasn't even saying anything, but I was rejoicing in my heart as I saw a person's head being healed on a You Tube video. A healing angel came on my sister's head as she walked by me. The rejoicing in my heart and the word of the Lord released non-verbally through the You Tube video, triggered angelic activity.

Another time, I told a friend *"Hey, I want to show you some videos."* We watched videos on You Tube of people ministering healing on the streets. I found a video of a guy praying for a women who had asked him for money. In the video, he prayed *"God, I ask for a wind to come in the natural, and blow around her head."*

The moment we heard this prayer in the You Tube video, we both felt a steady breeze begin blowing from my bedroom window. The bedroom window was a completely closed, airtight replacement window!

He continued praying, giving many accurate words of knowledge about the lady's health conditions. In the video, we saw the lady's hair blowing in the wind. Then we heard him pray *"God, double it!"*

At that moment, the breeze coming from the closed window in my bedroom instantly doubled. Again, there was a sense of God's peace in the wind.

You can imagine how these experiences impressed me with the importance of being careful about what is coming through the TV! I don't want to passively receive whatever comes to me. Rather, I should declare heavenly reality wherever I am, and say *"Shut up!"* to whatever the devil is proclaiming. Sometimes, that means changing the TV channel, or turning off the TV.

In fact, I never watched TV in my house during all my single years. For most of that time, I didn't even own one. It was too much of a distraction from the really important things. If I wanted to watch something, I went to my parent's house.

I'm not saying any of this to be legalistic. I'm encouraging you to be aware of what happens in the spirit realm and how real it is. Be honest with yourself about what is helpful to you, and what isn't. If something you're watching on TV is hurting you, turn it off!

I don't want to bring a proclamation into my house that agrees with the lies of demons. I prefer to have my house so full of thanksgiving to God and the proclamation of his glory that people are healed and see angels in my house.

Commanding Angels?

Some people talk about commanding God's angels to go and do their bidding. I personally don't see any support in scripture for Christians to command angels what to do. Neither do I see any need for us to command them. When I read the stories scripture records of people encountering angels, the idea of our telling them what to do seems dubious.

In my view, we don't need to command angels what to do. Rather, we declare God's word, and they respond to his word. They obey the Lord. Angels do respect the authority God has given men over his creation, and so they eagerly wait for us to add our *"Amen"* to God's *"Yes."*

I don't command angels. Instead, I say something like, *"In Jesus' name, may the peace of God fill your body right now. May the peace of God drive out everything that isn't in heaven."* I simply agree with what I already know is God's will. When I do so, the Lord usually chooses to minister his peace through an angelic messenger. People often tangibly feel something touching them. This happens regularly.

I have prayed for people many times by holding my hand six inches away from their body, or extending my hands towards them from even a greater distance. They've often felt a hand on their body when I was not touching them, sometimes even thinking my hand was actually on them. When I came into agreement with the Lord's will by extending my hands, an angel laid hands on them to minister. This has been a sign from the Lord for many people.

On one occasion I offered a guy a ride to the local rescue mission. As I was getting into my truck to leave, I saw a man on crutches. I jumped back out and talked with him, then I stood in front of him, extended my hands towards his knees, and said *"In Jesus' name, knees be healed"*.

Not only did the Lord touch his knees and the pain left, but he began to physically feel hands kneading and pressing on his knees. No human was touching him! He said *"The hands are pressing on my knees just like the physical therapist does!"*

Two more times, I was just getting in my truck and about to leave, and I saw a person who needed to be healed so I jumped back out! And the Lord touched both of them as well.

Thanking God For Testimonies Of Angels

The principle of *"drawing water from the wells of salvation"* applies to angelic activity. When people hear a report of the Holy Spirit's work, they may immediately experience the same healing. The angels take the testimony as the word of the Lord, and they respond to it.

When you hear reports or testimonies of angels, I encourage you thank the Lord for his works and for sending angels to help us. I would not at all be surprised if some people reading my testimonies of angels begin to have similar experiences.

Awareness of angelic activity is encouraging. It can also help us see what the Holy Spirit is doing, so we can partner with it. Some people have seen angels pointing out a specific person and showing how the Lord wanted to minister to them.

I'm only aware of having seen an angel once with my physical eyes, but I have often become aware of them in other ways. I've often felt God's presence touching my body in various places in order to show me where people needed healing. This was most likely an angel the Lord sent to help me. It was also the Holy Spirit, since the angel was carrying the presence of the Lord.

As you learn to bless the Lord at all times and proclaim his praise continually, you're likely to have experiences like the ones I've shared quite frequently. Angels love to praise God and they love when we declare who the Lord is!

7. Praise, Strength, Faith, Battle

Praise And Strength

Look at these two passages of scripture. The verse in Psalms is the verse Jesus quoted in the first passage.

Matthew 21:14-16 The blind and the lame came to him in the temple, and he cured them. But when the chief priests and the scribes saw the amazing things that he did, and heard the children crying out in the temple, "Hosanna to the Son of David," they became angry and said to him, "Do you hear what these are saying?" Jesus said to them, "Yes; have you never read, 'Out of the mouths of infants and nursing babies you have prepared praise for yourself'?"

Psalm 8:2 (ESV) Out of the mouth of babies and infants, you have established strength because of your foes, to still the enemy and the avenger.

Did you notice the word *"praise"* in the first passage we read and the word *"strength"* in the second passage? In both of these passages, some translations use the word *"strength"* and some use the word *"praise."* The Hebrew word used in Psalms 8:2 is usually translated in other places as *"power"* or *"strength."* Yet according to Strong's definition, part of the meaning of this word is *"praise."*[26] The context of Jesus quoting this verse in the New Testament also points to praise.

---

[26] Strong's Hebrew And Greek Dictionaries, Word H5797

Psalm 84 has been a great help to me and has lifted my spirit. Reading it and taking it to heart has led me to experience what it speaks of.

Psalm 84:4-7 Happy are those who live in your house, ever singing your praise. Selah. Happy are those whose strength is in you, in whose heart are the highways to Zion. As they go through the valley of Baca they make it a place of springs; the early rain also covers it with pools. They go from strength to strength; the God of gods will be seen in Zion.

The word *"Baca"* means *"weeping."* Some translations, such as the Young's Literal Translation and the Amplified version, say *"valley of weeping."* Those who are always singing God's praise have their strength in the Lord, and they will turn the valley of weeping into a place of springs. They will go from one degree of strength to another.

At times when I was discouraged or despondent, I was in a *"valley of weeping."* The Lord spoke to me through Psalm 84 and told me to turn the valley of weeping into a place of springs. And it worked! As I resolved to be *"ever singing God's praise"* I became so strong in the Lord it seemed my heart exploded with power. I felt nothing was impossible. I began to do exploits by the power of God.

Daniel 11:32 (ASV) ...but the people that know their God shall be strong, and do exploits.

Nehemiah 8:10 ...the joy of the Lord is your strength

I've also read Psalm 89 over and over again. This also speaks of constantly praising the Lord and become super-strong in him.

Psalm 89:15-17 Happy are the people who know the festal shout, who walk, O Lord, in the light of your countenance; they exult in your name all day long, and extol your righteousness. For you are the glory of their strength; by your favor our horn is exalted.

Again, Psalm 89 talks about exalting the name of the Lord all day long and extolling his righteousness. This is living in heaven while on earth! This is walking in the glory of the Lord, as heavenly people! You become strong in the Lord, strengthened by his glory. *"Horn"* in the Old Testament is symbolic of power. You will be exalted and made strong as you declare God's praise.

Ephesians 6:10 Finally, be strong in the Lord and in the strength of his power.

Ephesians 3:16 I pray that, according to the riches of his glory, he may grant that you may be strengthened in your inner being with power through his Spirit.

As you experience this inner strength, you will be constantly looking for ways to exercise the power of God that fills your being. Strength looks for expression.

I have often felt like this. When I feel strong, I look for something to push against. I look for a person who needs healing or deliverance. I look for a person who needs a heavy burden lifted. When you continually give thanks to the Lord you are motivated to keep speaking God's word and to never shut up, because miracles start to happen all around. You get busy crushing the works of the devil!

Jesus' Promises About Faith And Prayer

Jesus gave us incredible promises of what will be possible if we believe God and speak in faith. How seriously do we take his words?

Mark 11:23 "Truly I tell you, if you say to this mountain, 'Be taken up and thrown into the sea,' and if you do not doubt in your heart, but believe that what you say will come to pass, it will be done for you. So I tell you, whatever you ask for in prayer, believe that you have received it, and it will be yours."

1 John 5:14-15 And this is the boldness we have in him, that if we ask anything according to his will, he hears us. And if we know that he hears us in whatever we ask, we know that we have obtained the requests made of him.

All too often, when we pray or speak in Christ's name and don't get the desired outcome, we give just about any reason except, *"I didn't believe."* Yet the only reason Jesus ever gave in scripture for his disciples being unable to cast out a demon or heal someone was because of their unbelief.

Matthew 17:14-21 When they came to the crowd, a man came to him, knelt before him, and said, "Lord, have mercy on my son, for he is an epileptic and he suffers terribly; he often falls into the fire and often into the water. And I brought him to your disciples, but they could not cure him." Jesus answered, "You faithless and perverse generation, how much longer must I be with you? How much longer must I put up with you? Bring him here to me."

And Jesus rebuked the demon, and it came out of him, and the boy was cured instantly. Then the disciples came to Jesus privately and said, "Why could we not cast it out?" He said to them, "Because of your little faith. For truly I tell you, if you have faith the size of a mustard seed, you will say to this mountain, 'Move from here to there,' and it will move; and nothing will be impossible for you."

One of the reasons it's hard for some to accept this teaching of Jesus is because of painful experiences. People have been told it was their fault they were not healed because they didn't have faith.

However, the record of scripture shows us all the faith needed to receive healing or deliverance from Jesus, was to come to him. All the faith anyone should need in order to receive what the Lord wants to give them should be to come—to us, the body of Christ.

This passage, on the other hand, address *having faith to minister* to people who need to be set free from sickness or oppression. It's our job to believe and do the works of Jesus when people come to us.

It can still be a hard pill to swallow that someone we laid hands on was not healed or set free from oppression because of our unbelief. Many people don't even want to consider that. It hurts.

Yet take into account the fact that Jesus' disciples had already ministered with great success before this, healing sick people and casting out demons. They had probably already healed more sick people than many of us have! They had been so successful that Jesus rejoiced because he saw *"Satan fall like lightning from heaven."*[27] Yet when these same disciples were unable to cast out the demon and heal the boy who was

---

[27] Luke 10:18

tormented, Jesus told them it was because of their unbelief.

Jesus also cast out the demon and healed the boy, demonstrating not only that it was God's will, but also that it was possible for the disciples. Scripture is crystal clear about how important it is that we believe!

James 1:6-7 But ask in faith, never doubting, for the one who doubts is like a wave of the sea, driven and tossed by the wind; for the doubter, being double-minded and unstable in every way, must not expect to receive anything from the Lord.

If we take Jesus' words as true, it can be frustrating and difficult to deal with situations where we pray according to God's will, yet don't get the desired results. If our perspective isn't right, we may struggle with feelings of spiritual weakness or even guilt over not having been able to believe.

But what are the consequences of dismissing Jesus' words because they are hard to deal with? If we do, we nullify the marvelous scriptural promises of receiving in prayer. We miss out on wonderful victories that are possible for us in the Lord!

I have often heard *"I believed, but it didn't work."* However, this statement cannot logically be true, if Jesus' promise about faith was true. Jesus said if we believed, nothing would be impossible for us. So maybe we need to understand better what the faith is that Jesus was talking about.

Maybe we need to understand better what it looks like to *"believe in your heart."* I think we can find a perspective on faith that's in accordance with the promises of scripture and also encourages us. (Instead of making us feel frustrated.)

What Does Faith Look Like?

Faith is seeing God. It's being far more impressed with his presence than with anything else. We believe when God's glory fills the eyes of our hearts and becomes far greater in our perception than anything else we may face.

Often the reason people say *"I believed, but it didn't work,"* is because they're talking about believing in their minds. Jesus wasn't referring to mental acknowledgement, intellectual assent or mind power, but to faith in God. This kind of faith springs from the experiential knowledge of the Lord. It comes through relationship with God, and it grows as we grow in the knowledge of the Lord.

Jesus is the author and perfecter of our faith.[28] This should encourage us! Growing in faith corresponds to growing in grace and in the knowledge of the Lord. It corresponds to the eyes of our hearts being opened.

2 Peter 3:18 But grow in the grace and knowledge of our Lord and Savior Jesus Christ.

Colossians 1:10 ...so that you may lead lives worthy of the Lord, fully pleasing to him, as you bear fruit in every good work and as you grow in the knowledge of God.

All of us have room to grow, so it should not be a hard or heavy thing for us to consider that we have a need to grow in faith! We can grow in grace and become stronger in the Lord! Many have defined grace as *"unmerited favor."* However, the word *"grace"* in scripture often refers to God's ability to do what we cannot do. The grace of God empowers us to do exploits and miracles in Christ's name.

---

[28] Hebrews 12:2

How many times do we pray with our eyes on the problem, instead of on what the Holy Spirit is doing? How many times do we pray motivated by fear? I know I have far too many times.

The fact I have room to grow in faith encourages me. When I face a problem, I can do something about it. It is still possible, even if I haven't seen it yet!

What would be discouraging for me is the idea that *"Sometimes we just pray, and it doesn't work, and we don't know why."* If it were so, I would be left helpless. People tend to embrace such reasoning because they are uncomfortable considering their need to grow in faith and in grace. It sounds good to the carnal mind, but it's not scriptural.

Ephesians 4:15 (ASV) ...but speaking truth in love, may grow up in all things into him, who is the head, even Christ...

Ephesians 4:15 (NIV) Instead, speaking the truth in love, we will grow to become in every respect the mature body of him who is the head, that is, Christ.

Do *"in all things"* and *"in every respect"* include faith, grace, and power? I'm sure they do. How do we know when we have grown to become, in every respect, the mature body of Christ? It becomes evident when we, the church, do all that Jesus did. Everyone who touched Jesus was healed. When we have grown up in all things into Christ, everyone who touches us will be healed.

John 14:12 Very truly, I tell you, the one who believes in me will also do the works that I do and, in fact, will do greater works than these, because I am going to the Father.

Real faith is like being in heaven, because it is beholding the Lord. I've experienced it. When prayer *"doesn't work,"* I ask myself *"Have I grown up in all things into the full measure of the stature of Christ? Is my face shining brighter with God's glory than Moses' face was, right now? Am I walking as fully as possible in the peace found in heaven, free from anxiety, my attention consumed with the presence of the Lord? Is it possible for the glory and power of God to be demonstrated through my life to a greater degree than it is now? "*

The obvious answer is I have room to grow. Yes, it is possible for the glory of God to be demonstrated through my life to a greater degree than it is now, so everyone sees my face is radiant, and even those I walk by are healed by the overflow of the Lord's glory.

Not everyone I have ministered to has been delivered. I still have room to grow! Yet I have watched a dozen people laying hands on an injured man and praying fervently for a long time, but with their eyes on the injury. They got no results. They believed God healed, but didn't have any confidence it was always his time to heal. When they finally got tired, I laid my hands on the guy and spoke shortly, and he was healed.

This shows that just because something didn't happen, it doesn't mean it wasn't God's will. The Lord was looking for a person who would believe. I knew it was God's will to heal the man at that moment, and my perception had become straightened out enough so the presence of the Lord was bigger in the eyes of my heart than the injury. Faith is not *"hit or miss."* If you believe, nothing will be impossible for you.

We talked about laughing in the chapter on proclamation. Faith laughs, because it is so impressed with the Lord, and so expectant of what he is about to do. It laughs because it beholds the Lord, and everything else looks small in comparison.

Faith often feels like a strength that fills your heart as you behold the Lord's glory. I don't believe I have ever laid hands on someone in faith, without results.

However, there have often been times when the Lord showed me how I got out of a place of faith. He also helped me by straightening out my perspective and showing me what I could do to act in faith.

Sometimes after seeing many miracles, I began to expect something to happen based on natural knowledge. For example, many people's knees were healed, so I expected the same thing the next time.

At first I felt like I believed, but I had really gone back to having confidence in what I saw with my natural eyes, instead of in the goodness of the Lord. The feeling of faith was based on seeing so many knees healed before instead of based on trusting in God. So, what would happen if I were confronted with a situation I had never yet seen healed before? I would have had no confidence if I continued to look at only natural things.

Faith in God comes from knowing him. Many people believe in *"the power of faith"* and don't even know God. Their idea of faith is not *"confidence in God,"* but it is mind-power or will-power. It has no need of God.

Having your faith in the power of your mind, or *"mind over matter,"* is having misplaced confidence. Confidence not placed in the Lord is unbelief towards God.

Many people have tried to have faith and said *"It didn't work"* because their view of faith was one of *"mind over matter."* It wasn't any different than the faith of pantheists who believe everything is god. True faith in God requires a revelation of the goodness of God and a personal knowledge of him. Our faith in God grows as we get to know him better.

There have also been times when I didn't feel like I had faith, but I did. I felt weak in the natural sense. I didn't feel like I was mentally convinced the thing that needed to happen was going to happen. However, I had a revelation of God's goodness, and I knew it is his will to heal. Because of that, healing did happen. Although I felt naturally weak, I had confidence in God's goodness.

Praise And Faith

We read in Psalms 84 that those who are ever singing God's praise go from *"strength to strength."* Going from *"strength to strength"* corresponds with going from one degree of faith to another, and with going from *"glory to glory"* as we behold the glory of the Lord.[29] Look at how Abraham became strong in faith.

Romans 4:20 No distrust made him waver concerning the promise of God, but he grew strong in his faith as he gave glory to God

Some other versions say he grew strong in faith *"giving praise to God"* or *"giving thanks to God."* Resolve that you are going to believe God's words and sing his praise.

Psalm 106:12 Then they believed his words; they sang his praise.

Romans 10:17 (NKJV) So then faith comes by hearing, and hearing by the word of God

Singing God's praise and talking about his goodness and mighty works, are proclaiming God's word. If faith comes by hearing, then start proclaiming God's word to yourself. Tell your soul who the Lord is, and tell your

---

[29] 2 Corinthians 3:18

soul to bless the Lord. If you learn to be *"ever singing God's praise,"* you will go from glory to glory, strength to strength, and faith to faith.

Healed As I Was Singing

For the first few years after I started healing the sick, I still got colds like I always had. It was frustrating every time to get a cold, because I now knew it was God's will to heal me. Yet I continued laying hands on other people, because many other people were being healed.

The first time I was healed of a cold was before my second trip to Russia. I had already seen the Holy Spirit do wonderful things on my first trip, and I had been praying a lot for the second trip. My mind was full of testimonies I wanted to share. I was expecting to see the Lord heal many people.

But I got a bad cold and sore throat a few days before the trip. My throat was raw and hurt terribly. I was also physically exhausted after a week of hard roofing work and not enough sleep.

Getting a cold was frustrating! I was planning to go to Russia to talk about God's healing power, and I was sick! I felt the fear I'd be like this for two weeks and it would make the beginning of my trip to Russia miserable.

But the Lord spoke to me about refusing to accept the fear that came with having a cold. Even though I knew I wasn't going to die from the cold, I realized even the fear of suffering with this for two weeks was a form of the fear of death. Jesus came to set me free from that!

Hebrews 2:14-15 Since, therefore, the children share flesh and blood, he himself likewise shared the same things, so that through death he might destroy the one who has the power of death, that is, the devil, and free those who all their lives were held in slavery by the fear of death.

It was a Friday night, and a travelling ministry was holding a worship conference at our church that weekend. I was leaving for Russia on Sunday. In a natural sense, the best thing to do when exhausted and sick would be to sleep. But I didn't care. I wanted so much to go to the Friday night meeting and sing to the Lord, that I went anyways.

As I sang, my heart flooded with thanksgiving to the Lord for saving me and for all he had done for me. My mind was full of scriptures about all we have in Christ, and the glory of them overwhelmed my soul. I sang with all my heart, sore throat and all.

As I sang and lifted my hands, I felt my lips and hands begin vibrating, and it was hard to stand up straight because I could feel the Lord's glory on me like a weight. This vibration spread in my body and become extremely strong. My upper body was vibrating with a violent force, and of course, I was weeping. Here I was, experiencing something very tangible and very supernatural, but my throat was still sore.

I thought, *"How is it possible for me to experience the Lord's glory in such a powerful way, and still have a sore throat?"* But I focused on the Lord and forgot about the sore throat.

It was pretty late when the meeting ended. I think it was about 11:00 pm. After everything finished, I stayed hanging out and talking to people. Within 15 minutes after I had finished singing, all the symptoms were gone!

Heaven is heaven because God is there, and when we experience his presence we encounter an order in which no sickness can exist. When we face a battle, the best thing to do is turn up the heat by declaring God's praise until there's such a manifestation of his glory that the mountains melt like wax!

My attention became so consumed with the Lord that I didn't care about the cold anymore. The fact my throat felt sore as I was singing didn't matter.

Throughout the next few weeks, there were several times I felt an itch in my throat, and the voice of fear spoke to my mind, telling me I was catching a cold again. Each time I refused it, declaring *"Jesus came to set me free from the fear of death!"*

I continued declaring the Lord's goodness without ceasing, and experienced one of the most glorious periods of time I have ever known. I often felt like I was walking in heaven. I didn't get sick again, and I experienced miracles and many supernatural manifestations of the Lord's glory on that trip, in both New York City and Russia.

I can't say I have never gotten a cold since then. Yet several times since then I've started to get a cold, but I went to a meeting and sang to the Lord until the symptoms were gone. Many people won't go to church if they have a cold. I began to think *"The assembly of the saints should be the place we go because we are sick!"*

I do know I encountered something that's possible to experience all the time. I tasted of a glorious reality in which we can live immune to sickness because the Lord's light shines so brightly through us as we declare his praise, that nothing which isn't in heaven can exist in our bodies.

As I sang, declaring the Lord's goodness, the very atmosphere began to vibrate with the reality of what I was declaring. Heaven's reality became manifest on earth, as a man with dominion on the earth declared the word about God's nature. The word about Christ has real substance.

Psalm 22:3 Yet you are holy, enthroned on the praises of Israel.

In the third book of this series, *Jesus Has Come In The Flesh*, we examine the important truth that God gave dominion over the earth to human beings. For now, it's sufficient to say that God gave mankind dominion over creation and God's dominion on the earth is established when men proclaim his praise.

Imagine what is possible if we determine to be found *"ever praising"* the Lord, so we go from strength to strength and glory to glory! It is more than we could have ever asked or imagined![30]

Standing Against Fear And Breast Cancer Disappearing

This happened on a Sunday night at my parent's house. There was a small gathering of people there, united to worship the Lord, share from scripture, and pray for each other.

A friend of ours was there who had an extremely difficult family situation. A loved one had been kidnapped and brainwashed. It was heartbreaking to hear what she was confronting and hard to imagine the stress she must have felt. She also had a cancerous tumor on her breast, which she said was the size of a child's fist.

We gathered around her to pray. I sat on the couch on the other side of the room. I prayed a lot in tongues. Then when my turn came, I prayed using scriptures applicable to her situation.

As I sat there praying, my heart was bursting with God's love and I felt a current of power flowing out of my hand towards her. I knew she had breast cancer, but

---

[30] Ephesians 3:20

I sensed the Holy Spirit first wanted us to deal with her situation.

After we prayed for the family situation, it was time to deal with the breast cancer. She told us that when we prayed for her family situation, she felt heat resting on the area where the tumor was. I asked her to put her hand on her breast. Then I held my palm about a foot in front of her and began to curse the tumor and release the goodness of God in her body. *"In Jesus' name, tumor go and everything be made whole".*

She felt a powerful manifestation of heat and energy in her body. However, I had laid my hands on people with cancer before who felt a manifestation of the Holy Spirit but later died, or else needed surgery. Because of this I felt the fear she would feel God's touch, but afterwards not recover completely and need surgery and chemotherapy.

Fear is attached to situations like cancer, and I was feeling that fear. Of course I didn't want the fear, and I tried to focus on what the Lord was doing instead. Sometimes people ask why it seems so easy for knees and backs to be healed, but not diseases like cancer. It is logical for us to understand that cancer is not any harder for God to heal. Neither is healing cancer any less God's will than healing a knee. So why does it seem like it is harder than healing a knee or a headache?

The answer is in understanding how God works. It is *"according to his power at work within us."*[31] More fear is attached to problems like cancer. If we are going to *"exercise dominion in life"*[32] over cancer, we must let God's perfect love cast out all fear,[33] so the *"peace of*

---

[31] Ephesians 3:20 (NIV)
[32] Romans 5:17
[33] 1 John 4:18

94

God which passes understanding "[34] rules in our hearts.[35] When we are free from fear, destroying cancer is as easy as healing a knee.

Before I had a solid scriptural foundation to go on or started to see miracles happen, I tried to step out and do exploits a few times, with poor results. I said something that sounded bold, but my heart was trembling. I was trying to work up faith because I desperately wanted to see God do something. The results were discouraging.

However, when I became convinced it was always God's will to heal, I knew I could at least say *"God wants to heal you right now,"* and be confident it was true. *Saying "God is going to heal you right now"* was still a big step. I couldn't yet say that with confidence. Yet I often said *"God wants to heal you right now"* to people, and many were healed.

When I began to get words of knowledge, I became bolder. If I discerned somebody had a particular problem I'd ask a question. For example, I would ask *"Do you have pain in your kidneys?"* When they said *"yes,"* that gave me the confidence to say *"God is going to heal your kidneys right now."* I wasn't trying to work up faith. I was confident of it.

As I continued to declare God's praise and experience his mighty works, it even got to the point where I would say *"God is going to heal you right now"* without getting a word of knowledge. As my heart was strengthened by the Holy Spirit, I had the confidence to say that. It was like a fact to me. If I wasn't confident of something, I knew because my heart trembled. It was better to say *"God wants to heal you right now,"* unless I knew I could say *"You are going to be healed right now"* with no fear.

---

[34] Philippians 4:7
[35] Colossians 3:15

Our friend felt a powerful manifestation of the Holy Spirit, yet I struggled with the fear that even though she felt heat and electricity the cancer would not be fully gone. Then the Holy Spirit spoke to me and said *"Tell her when she checks for the cancer, it won't be there anymore."*

This was a bold thing to say, but to stand firm against the fear, I needed to say this to her. I obeyed the Lord and I told her *"Don't worry. When you feel for it again, try to find it and it won't be there."* I could feel the power of God in my words.

She went to the bathroom and felt where the tumor was. She still felt it but it was much smaller. When she told me, it felt as if my heart was bursting with strength, strengthened by the love of God, and I was confident. I wasn't deterred. I said *"Don't worry. Check again in a little while and it will be gone."*

Five minutes later she checked again, on the way to her car. She couldn't feel the tumor at all, which before had been the size of a child's fist. The cancer was gone! Thank you Jesus!

Earlier, we talked about singing the Lord's praise before the *"gods."* False gods try to capture our attention through fear. We must refuse fear, and instead sing the Lord's praise. Cancer is a false god. It wants to get our attention and become bigger in our perception than the Lord is, but we must refuse it.

When we face cancer, our motivation to pray must never be fear of the cancer. All too often, Christians *"pray harder"* about certain circumstances because they are afraid. Then when they don't see something healed that Jesus would have healed, they say *"Everyone prayed, but it didn't work."*

If fear is motivating our prayers, we aren't in a place of faith. We must come to the place where our hearts are so strengthened by the Holy Spirit that our vision of the Lord's glory is what motivates our prayers, and never fear.

Going To Battle

The name *"Judah"* means *"praise."* When the Israelites were going to battle and asked the Lord who to send first, the Lord said to send the tribe of Judah.

Judges 1:1-2 After the death of Joshua, the Israelites inquired of the LORD, "Who shall go up first for us against the Canaanites, to fight against them?" The LORD said, "Judah shall go up. I hereby give the land into his hand."

The first city the Israelites encountered as they entered the Promised Land was Jericho. Remember how they overcame this city?

Joshua 6:12-16, 20 Then Joshua rose early in the morning, and the priests took up the ark of the LORD. The seven priests carrying the seven trumpets of rams' horns before the ark of the LORD passed on, blowing the trumpets continually. The armed men went before them, and the rear guard came after the ark of the LORD, while the trumpets blew continually. On the second day they marched around the city once and then returned to the camp. They did this for six days.

    On the seventh day they rose early, at dawn, and marched around the city in the same manner seven times. It was only on that day that they marched around the city seven times. And at the seventh time, when the priests had blown the trumpets, Joshua said to the people, "Shout! For the LORD has given you the city...

    So the people shouted, and the trumpets were blown. As soon as the people heard the sound of the trumpets, they raised a great shout, and the wall fell down flat; so the people charged straight ahead into the city and captured it.

I think it's clear that the trumpets or shofars, and the shout, are forms of proclamation. According to Jewish tradition, the shofar says, *"Awake, sleepers from your sleep, and slumberers arise from your slumber!"*[36] Scripture also connects the trumpet blast to resurrection.[37]

Ephesians 5:13-14 ...everything exposed by the light becomes visible, for everything that becomes visible is light. Therefore it says, "Sleeper, awake! Rise from the dead, and Christ will shine on you."

Isaiah 26:19 Your dead shall live, their corpses shall rise. O dwellers in the dust, awake and sing for joy! For your dew is a radiant dew, and the earth will give birth to those long dead.

Isaiah 60:1-3 Arise, shine; for your light has come, and the glory of the LORD *has risen upon you. For darkness shall cover the earth, and thick darkness the peoples; but the* LORD *will arise upon you, and his glory will appear over you. Nations shall come to your light, and kings to the brightness of your dawn.*

The fact that the priests marching around Jericho blew seven trumpets reminds me of the *"seven spirits of God"* and God's seven *"redemptive names"* which we talked about. I like to think of the blowing of seven trumpets as symbolic of declaring the various aspects of God's character in praise; declaring the seven names of the Lord.

---

[36]http://www.divreinavon.com/pdf/Anticipation_Consummation.pdf
[37] 1 Corinthians 15:52, 1 Thessalonians 4:16

We *"awaken the dawn"* and call those who are spiritually dead to life, as we proclaim God's praise and shout with the joy of salvation. By doing so, we take cities that were in bondage to darkness as our inheritance. They will become filled with the knowledge of God's glory!

Proverbs 21:22 (NLV) A wise man goes over the city walls of the powerful, and brings down the strong-place in which they trust.

Matthew 5:5 "Blessed are the meek, for they will inherit the earth.

Psalm 37:29 The righteous shall inherit the land, and live in it forever.

Praise and proclamation also go with victory in battle in other Old Testament stories. Gideon and his three-hundred men defeated the vast army of the Midianites with shouts and trumpet blasts.[38] The Midianites had been oppressing Israel. We also are delivered from oppression as we release the light of the knowledge of God's glory through our declaration.

Later in Israel's history, a large army threatened them again— this time of Moabites, Ammonites, and Meunites. King Jehoshaphat proclaimed a fast, and he and all Judah assembled to seek the Lord. Jehoshaphat prayed:

2 Chronicles 20:5-7, Jehoshaphat stood in the assembly of Judah and Jerusalem, in the house of the LORD, before the new court, and said, "O LORD, God of our ancestors, are you not God in heaven? Do you not rule over all the

---

[38] Judges 6 and 7

kingdoms of the nations? In your hand are power and might, so that no one is able to withstand you. Did you not, O our God, drive out the inhabitants of this land before your people Israel, and give it forever to the descendants of your friend Abraham?...For we are powerless against this great multitude that is coming against us. We do not know what to do, but our eyes are on you."

Notice that in his prayer, Jehoshaphat declared God's rule over the nations of the earth and proclaimed his power. Then he declared how the Lord had delivered them before. He prayed with praise and thanksgiving.

2 Chronicles 20:14-30 Then the spirit of the LORD came upon Jahaziel son of Zechariah, son of Benaiah, son of Jeiel, son of Mattaniah, a Levite of the sons of Asaph, in the middle of the assembly. He said, "Listen, all Judah and inhabitants of Jerusalem, and King Jehoshaphat: Thus says the LORD to you: 'Do not fear or be dismayed at this great multitude; for the battle is not yours but God's.

Tomorrow go down against them; they will come up by the ascent of Ziz; you will find them at the end of the valley, before the wilderness of Jeruel. This battle is not for you to fight; take your position, stand still, and see the victory of the LORD on your behalf, O Judah and Jerusalem.' Do not fear or be dismayed; tomorrow go out against them, and the LORD will be with you.

Then Jehoshaphat bowed down with his face to the ground, and all Judah and the inhabitants of Jerusalem fell down before the LORD, worshiping the LORD. And the Levites, of the Kohathites and the Korahites, stood up to praise the LORD, the God of Israel, with a very loud voice.

They rose early in the morning and went out into the wilderness of Tekoa; and as they went out, Jehoshaphat stood and said, "Listen to me, O Judah and inhabitants of Jerusalem! Believe in the LORD your God and you will be established; believe his prophets." When he had taken counsel with the people, he appointed those who were to sing to the LORD and praise him in holy splendor, as they went before the army, saying,

"Give thanks to the LORD, for his steadfast love endures forever."

As they began to sing and praise, the LORD set an ambush against the Ammonites, Moab, and Mount Seir, who had come against Judah, so that they were routed. For the Ammonites and Moab attacked the inhabitants of Mount Seir, destroying them utterly; and when they had made an end of the inhabitants of Seir, they all helped to destroy one another.

When Judah came to the watchtower of the wilderness, they looked toward the multitude; they were corpses lying on the ground; no one had escaped. When Jehoshaphat and his people came to take the booty from them, they found livestock in great numbers, goods, clothing, and precious things, which they took for themselves until they could carry no more. They spent three days taking the booty, because of its abundance.

On the fourth day they assembled in the Valley of Beracah, for there they blessed the LORD; therefore that place has been called the Valley of Beracah to this day. Then all the people of Judah and Jerusalem, with Jehoshaphat at their head, returned to Jerusalem with joy, for the LORD had enabled them to rejoice over their enemies. They came to Jerusalem, with harps and lyres and trumpets, to the house of the LORD.

The fear of God came on all the kingdoms of the countries when they heard that the LORD had fought against the enemies of Israel. And the realm of

Jehoshaphat was quiet, for his God gave him rest all around.

Remember when we talked about singing the Lord's praise before the *"gods"*? Many things will try to capture our attention through fear — the attention only the Lord is worthy of. We refuse to fear or give them attention as we praise our Lord. This is how we overcome them. Faith is having your attention captured by the Lord.

Just as we read in 2 Chronicles 20 that the battle was the Lord's, Isaiah also talks about the Lord himself fighting as people declare his praise with singing and musical instruments.

Isaiah 30:29-32. You shall have a song as in the night when a holy festival is kept; and gladness of heart, as when one sets out to the sound of the flute to go to the mountain of the LORD, to the Rock of Israel.

And the LORD will cause his majestic voice to be heard and the descending blow of his arm to be seen, in furious anger and a flame of devouring fire, with a cloudburst and tempest and hailstones. The Assyrian will be terror-stricken at the voice of the LORD, when he strikes with his rod.

And every stroke of the staff of punishment that the LORD lays upon him will be to the sound of timbrels and lyres; battling with brandished arm he will fight with him.

Isaiah 42:10-13 Sing to the LORD a new song, his praise from the end of the earth! Let the sea roar and all that fills it, the coastlands and their inhabitants.

Let the desert and its towns lift up their voice, the villages that Kedar inhabits; let the inhabitants of Sela sing for joy, let them shout from the tops of the mountains.

Let them give glory to the LORD, and declare his praise in the coastlands. The LORD goes forth like a soldier, like a warrior he stirs up his fury; he cries out, he shouts aloud, he shows himself mighty against his foes.

8. Praise And Present Salvation

Confessing Jesus Is Lord

In the first book, *Present Access To Heaven*, we talked about salvation in the past, present, and future. We applied the passage of Romans 10 not only to being born again, but to salvation in the present.

Romans 10:8-10 "The word is near you, on your lips and in your heart" (that is, the word of faith that we proclaim); because if you confess with your lips that Jesus is Lord and believe in your heart that God raised him from the dead, you will be saved. For one believes with the heart and so is justified, and one confesses with the mouth and so is saved.

It's important we confess Jesus' Lordship with our mouths and believe in our hearts that God has raised him from the dead. What is confessing with our mouth that Jesus is Lord? It is proclaiming who God is, and therefore it is praise! The name *"Jesus"* means *"God Saves."* We declare God's salvation as we thank him for what he has done, and praise him by declaring who he is. We have applied this to being born again, but we can also apply it to present deliverance.

I've recounted my deliverance from a cold and sore throat as I declared the Lord's goodness and thanked him for saving me before. God's present salvation applies to all kinds of circumstances. It establishes the peace of heaven in every situation.

Many Christians have been born again, but struggle with sin and feelings of guilt and condemnation. The devil would like us to forget the work the Holy Spirit has already done in our lives.

If you struggle in this way, it's effective to thank and praise the Lord for what he's previously done in your life. Thank him for giving you a new heart and for forgiving you! Thank him for the gift of righteousness! Recount every time the Lord has delivered you in the past, and thank him for it!

I have had to do this often. At times, I felt I had failed terribly and was tormented with feelings of guilt and shame. However, as I thanked the Lord for what he'd done in my life, I once again knew God's deliverance from the power of sin. I felt a burden lift from my shoulders as the oppression left.

Thank God for his deliverance and declare his salvation. As you do this, you refocus on what the Holy Spirit is doing to help you. This gets your eyes off of yourself and your failures. Silence the accuser by declaring God's praise in the name of Jesus, *"God saves."* Jesus is Lord! God's salvation trumps all! It is greater than the power of sin, greater than my failures, and greater than anything which can come against me!

Psalm 50:23 (WEB) Whoever offers the sacrifice of thanksgiving glorifies me, and prepares his way so that I will show God's salvation to him.

Psalm 50:23 (WYC) The sacrifice of praising shall honour me; and there is the way, wherein I shall show to him the health of God.

Psalm 69:30-31 I will praise the name of God with a song; I will magnify him with thanksgiving. This will please the LORD more than an ox or a bull with horns and hoofs.

Hebrews 13:15 (NIV) Through Jesus, therefore, let us continually offer to God a sacrifice of praise—the fruit of lips that openly profess his name.

Deliverance From Prison

"Present salvation" applies to physical healing and deliverance from the power of sin and demonic oppression. It can also apply to being saved in unique, practical ways in the situations we face.

Acts 16:16-34 One day, as we were going to the place of prayer, we met a slave-girl who had a spirit of divination and brought her owners a great deal of money by fortune-telling. While she followed Paul and us, she would cry out, "These men are slaves of the Most High God, who proclaim to you a way of salvation."

She kept doing this for many days. But Paul, very much annoyed, turned and said to the spirit, "I order you in the name of Jesus Christ to come out of her." And it came out that very hour.

But when her owners saw that their hope of making money was gone, they seized Paul and Silas and dragged them into the marketplace before the authorities. When they had brought them before the magistrates, they said, "These men are disturbing our city; they are Jews and are advocating customs that are not lawful for us as Romans to adopt or observe."

The crowd joined in attacking them, and the magistrates had them stripped of their clothing and ordered them to be beaten with rods. After they had given them a severe flogging, they threw them into prison and ordered the jailer to keep them securely. Following these instructions, he put them in the innermost cell and fastened their feet in the stocks.

About midnight Paul and Silas were praying and singing hymns to God, and the prisoners were listening to them. Suddenly there was an earthquake, so violent that the foundations of the prison were shaken; and immediately all the doors were opened and everyone's chains were unfastened.

When the jailer woke up and saw the prison doors wide open, he drew his sword and was about to kill himself, since he supposed that the prisoners had escaped. But Paul shouted in a loud voice, "Do not harm yourself, for we are all here." The jailer called for lights, and rushing in, he fell down trembling before Paul and Silas. Then he brought them outside and said, "Sirs, what must I do to be saved?"

They answered, "Believe on the Lord Jesus, and you will be saved, you and your household." They spoke the word of the Lord to him and to all who were in his house. At the same hour of the night he took them and washed their wounds; then he and his entire family were baptized without delay. He brought them up into the house and set food before them; and he and his entire household rejoiced that he had become a believer in God.

This story is such an inspiration to me! Being stripped of clothing and beaten with rods is a horrible thing. Yet it could not stop these two believers from singing hymns to God.

Paul and Silas were not wallowing in self-pity! Their eyes were still on what the Holy Spirit was doing. They were willing and ready to partner with him! Even when they were miraculously released, they didn't flee to save their own skins. Instead, they were sensitive to the need of the jailer. The whole situation ended in salvation not only for them, but for the jailer and his entire household!

One of the lessons Corrie Ten Boom relates in *The Hiding Place*, is that a person who loves is free. No walls can shut them in. Corrie first learned this by watching her mother, before she and Betsie were ever in a concentration camp. Corrie's mother became immobile because of a stroke. But her love took her into all the world.

Mama's love had always been the kind that acted itself out with soup pot and sewing basket. But now that these things were taken away, the love seemed as whole as before. She sat in her chair at the window and loved us. She loved the people she saw in the street— and beyond: her love took in the city, the land of Holland, the world. And so I learned that love is larger than the walls that shut it in.[39]

Such freedom is in God's presence that Paul and Silas rejoiced in the freedom they had, even physically bound. As they rejoiced in a heavenly reality superseding their natural circumstances, the earth itself shook with the manifestation of God's glory until even the physical chains could not restrain them.

Provision

Mark 8:1-9 In those days when there was again a great crowd without anything to eat, he called his disciples and said to them, "I have compassion for the crowd, because they have been with me now for three days and have nothing to eat. If I send them away hungry to their

---

[39] Boom, Corrie Ten; Elizabeth Sherrill; John Sherrill (2006-01-01). The Hiding Place (p. 64). Baker Publishing Group. Kindle Edition.

homes, they will faint on the way—and some of them have come from a great distance." His disciples replied, "How can one feed these people with bread here in the desert?"

He asked them, "How many loaves do you have?" They said, "Seven." Then he ordered the crowd to sit down on the ground; and he took the seven loaves, and after giving thanks he broke them and gave them to his disciples to distribute; and they distributed them to the crowd. They had also a few small fish; and after blessing them, he ordered that these too should be distributed. They ate and were filled; and they took up the broken pieces left over, seven baskets full. Now there were about four thousand people. And he sent them away.

Remember the healing of Christina's eyes? As I gave testimony of the slight improvement for a blind lady, my sister received perfect eyesight. This is the same principle. Even though the need is far greater than what we have, we thank God for what we have. Jesus thanked God for seven loaves and a few small fish, even though there were four thousand people to feed.

Here's another quote from *The Hiding Place*. As Betsie Ten Boom taught Corrie to give thanks to God in everything (even in a concentration camp), they witnessed a miracle similar to those in biblical accounts.

ANOTHER STRANGE THING was happening. The Davitamon bottle was continuing to produce drops. It scarcely seemed possible, so small a bottle, so many doses a day.

Now, in addition to Betsie, a dozen others on our pier were taking it. My instinct was always to hoard it— Betsie was growing so very weak! But others were ill as well. It was hard to say no to eyes that burned with fever, hands that shook with chill.

I tried to save it for the very weakest— but even these soon numbered fifteen, twenty, twenty-five. . . . And still, every time I tilted the little bottle, a drop appeared at the top of the glass stopper. It just couldn't be! I held it up to the light, trying to see how much was left, but the dark brown glass was too thick to see through.

"There was a woman in the Bible," Betsie said, "whose oil jar was never empty." She turned to it in the Book of Kings, the story of the poor widow of Zarephath who gave Elijah a room in her home: "The jar of meal wasted not, neither did the cruse of oil fail, according to the word of Jehovah which he spoke by Elijah."

Well— but— wonderful things happened all through the Bible. It was one thing to believe that such things were possible thousands of years ago, another to have it happen now, to us, this very day. And yet it happened, this day, and the next, and the next, until an awed little group of spectators stood around watching the drops fall onto the daily rations of bread.

Many nights I lay awake in the shower of straw dust from the mattress above, trying to fathom the marvel of supply lavished upon us. "Maybe," I whispered to Betsie, "only a molecule or two really gets through that little pinhole— and then in the air it expands!" I heard her soft laughter in the dark. "Don't try too hard to explain it, Corrie. Just accept it as a surprise from a Father who loves you."[40]

My grandparents also experienced multiplication of food when my grandfather gave thanks to God for the little food they had. They were missionaries living in Belem

---

[40] Boom, Corrie Ten; Elizabeth Sherrill; John Sherrill (2006-01-01). The Hiding Place (p. 213-214). Baker Publishing Group. Kindle Edition.

do Para, Brazil. This was in the '70's, when my dad was a teenager. Their house was in front of the airstrip where Bible translators arrived from the jungle. After the airplanes full of missionaries arrived the newcomers went to my grandparents' house for dinner.

Ham was a rare and expensive commodity at that time in Brazil, but someone had brought a two pound canned ham from the US and given it to my grandparents as a Thanksgiving gift. That Thanksgiving, an airplane arrived on the airstrip. My grandparents had about fourteen guests, besides their own family. For about twenty people, there was very little food! Grammy said to Pappy, *"How are we going to feed all of these people?"*

Grammy told me that he looked at her and she saw in his eyes that he was full of faith. He said, *"Just cut it up and give it to them."*

After thanking the Lord for the food, they passed the plate around. Everyone had firsts. They passed it around again, and everyone had seconds. They passed the plate again, and some people had thirds. After everyone had finished, there was still enough ham left over for them to make ham sandwiches for the next few days. It was remarkable a 2 pound ham in a can could feed so many people!

Philippians 4:4-6 Rejoice in the Lord always; again I will say, Rejoice. Let your gentleness be known to everyone. The Lord is near. Do not worry about anything, but in everything by prayer and supplication with thanksgiving let your requests be made known to God.

Scripture teaches us to continually rejoice and make our needs known to God with thanksgiving. On my second trip to Russia, I was constantly rejoicing in the Lord and giving thanks to him. I experienced an interesting miracle of provision.

I was going, with my girlfriend, to preach to some people in a home in St. Petersburg. We were running late, but we only had one metro token left. There was a long line to buy metro tokens. We would be waiting a long time in line if we had to buy tokens, and would arrive very late.

However, a coin fell in front of us as we walked into the metro, seemingly out of thin air. Somebody picked it up and gave it to my girlfriend. We both asked *"Where did that come from?"* Then she said to me *"Jonathan, this is a miracle!"* We were able to get on the metro train without waiting in line, and arrived only a little late.

I thought this might have been a miracle, but I still wasn't sure there wasn't a natural explanation. Maybe we didn't see where the coin came from.

A few months after I returned from Russia, I went on a two-week trip to Maryland. When I got back, my housemates told me they thought angels were in my house and on my porch. This was when they told me *"weird, but good"* things were happening in my house.

One of my friends had been sitting alone on the steps of the front porch. He had his hand resting naturally open on his knee. Suddenly, a quarter fell directly into his hand out of thin air! Nobody else was around.

I was puzzled by this, but I had no reason to disbelieve my friend. This time, there was no possible natural explanation for the coin appearing out of thin air. But why? It was only a quarter, and it wasn't like it was meeting some great need. Yet it seemed to bless my friend.

I could see how God could have done this to reveal his generous nature to my friend. Looking back on this occurrence, I wonder if it was also meant to convince me the metro token incident really was a miracle! We read in scripture about Jesus having Peter take a coin out of a fish's mouth,[41] so why not a metro token falling out of thin air?

---

[41] Matthew 17:27

9. Give Thanks In Everything

Prayer With Thanksgiving

In the last chapter we read the exhortation of Philippians 4:6 to make our requests known to God with thanksgiving. In scripture, we regularly see the prayer of faith going hand-in-hand with praise and thanksgiving.

1 Thessalonians 5:16-18 Rejoice always, pray without ceasing, give thanks in all circumstances; for this is the will of God in Christ Jesus for you.

Ephesians 5:18-20 Do not get drunk with wine, for that is debauchery; but be filled with the Spirit, as you sing psalms and hymns and spiritual songs among yourselves, singing and making melody to the Lord in your hearts, giving thanks to God the Father at all times and for everything in the name of our Lord Jesus Christ.

The first passage tells us to give thanks in all circumstances. No matter the situation, we can be thankful because the Holy Spirit is working. We can give thanks to God because we are in heaven, surrounded by his presence.

The second passage tells us to give thanks at all times and *"for everything."* Singing and continually giving thanks to the Lord are related to being filled with the Holy Spirit. Can we really give God praise for everything? Even evil things?

A Vision About Praise

Soon after my experience in Belize, a lady told me about a guy named Merlin Carothers. I was talking so much about praise that she said I had to read Merlin's books.

Merlin joined the army during World War II and later became a believer and an army chaplain. He wrote several books about praise. They include testimonies of miracles which happened when people learned to thank God for things they were unhappy about. This excerpt from his book *Power In Praise* relates a vision he saw.

While I sat in the back of the auditorium during a healing service, I closed my eyes and on the screen of my inner vision God painted a picture.

I saw a beautiful, bright summer day. The air was filled with light, and I had a sense of everything being very beautiful. Up above was a heavy, solid black cloud beyond which nothing could be seen. A ladder extended from the ground up into the black cloud.

At the base of the ladder were hundreds of people trying to get a chance at climbing the ladder. They had heard that above the blackness there was something more beautiful than anything a human eye had ever seen, something that brought unbelievable joy to those who reached it. As person after person tried to ascend they quickly climbed to the lower edge of the clouds.

The crowd watched to see what would happen. In a short while the person would come wildly sliding down the ladder and fall into the crowd scattering people in all directions. They reported that once they got into the blackness they lost all sense of direction.

My time finally came, and as I made my way up the ladder into the blackness it grew so intense that I could feel its power nearly forcing me to give up and slide back. But step by step I continued upward until suddenly my eyes beheld the most intense brightness I had ever seen. It was a brilliant whiteness too glorious to describe in words.

As I came out above the dark cloud I realized that I could walk on top of it. As I looked into the brightness I was able to walk without difficulty. When I looked down to examine the nature of the cloud I immediately began to sink. Only by looking at the brightness could I stay on top. Then the scene changed and I was back looking at all three levels from a distance.

"What does it all mean?" I asked, and the answer came: "The brightest sunshine below the cloud is the light that many Christians live in and accept as normal. The ladder is the ladder of praising Me.

Many try to climb and learn to praise Me in all things. At first they are very eager, but when they get into things that they don't understand they become confused and cannot hold on. They lose faith and go sliding back. As they fall, they injure other people who have been hoping to find a way to live in continual joy and praise.

"Those who make it through those difficult times reach a new world and realize that the life they once thought of as normal cannot be compared to the life I have prepared for those who praise Me and believe that I carefully watch over them.

He who reaches the light of the heavenly kingdom can walk on top of difficulties no matter how dark they may seem as long as he keeps his eyes off the problem and on My victory in Christ. No matter how difficult it may seem to trust Me to work in every detail of your life, keep clinging to the ladder of praise and move upwards!"

I was half-dazed by the vision and the explanation and wondered how soon God would let me share it with someone. At the camp I met a woman who was faced with problems of illness and family difficulties at home. She found it hard to believe that praising God was going to do any good.

Inwardly I asked for guidance, and God said, "Tell her!" So I told her. "You'll be the first one to hear this," I said, and as she listened I could see how the heaviness literally left and her face and eyes lit up with a look of joyous expectancy.

In Ephesians, chapters one and two, I found my vision described in slightly different words by Paul: "...Blessed (Praised!) be the God and Father of our Lord Jesus Christ, who hath blessed us with all spiritual blessings in heavenly places in Christ: . . .he hath chosen us in him before the foundation of the world, that we should be holy and without blame. . .To the praise of the glory of his grace. . .that in. . .the fullness of times he might gather together in one all things in Christ. . .That we should be to the praise of his glory, who first trusted in Christ. . .that you may know. . .what is the exceeding greatness of his power to us-ward who believe, according to the working of his mighty power, which he wrought in Christ, when he raised him from the dead and set him at his own right hand in the heavenly places, Far above all principality and power, and might, and dominion. . .And hath raised us up together, and made us sit together in heavenly places in Christ Jesus."

Jesus Christ is raised above all the powers of darkness, and according to God's word, our rightful inheritance is right there above the darkness together in Christ. The ladder is praise![42]

Mr. Carothers had a wonderful revelation about praising and thanking God in everything. This is how to walk as a heavenly person; in heaven and on earth at the same

---

[42] Carothers, Merlin (1970-06-01). Prison To Praise (Kindle Locations 1129-1164). Merlin Carothers. Kindle Edition.

time! Notice how his description of the dark cloud fits so closely with my understanding of the *"spirit of heaviness"* and the *"thick darkness"* of Isaiah 60.

You'll enjoy *Prison To Praise* and Mr. Carothers' other books, if you get a chance to read them. Testimonies and encouragement fill their pages. Even though I have a different view of God's sovereignty than Mr. Carothers did, I believe his understanding about praising the Lord in and for everything is a treasure.

God Makes It Work For Good!

God is not the author of evil. God doesn't plan everything that happens, and many things happen which are not his will. Yet the Holy Spirit is an expert at taking what Satan meant for evil, and turning it around for good. Joseph was sold into slavery by his own brothers. That was a terrible thing! But look at what Joseph said:

Genesis 45:4-8 Then Joseph said to his brothers, "Come closer to me." And they came closer. He said, "I am your brother, Joseph, whom you sold into Egypt. And now do not be distressed, or angry with yourselves, because you sold me here; for God sent me before you to preserve life. For the famine has been in the land these two years; and there are five more years in which there will be neither plowing nor harvest.

God sent me before you to preserve for you a remnant on earth, and to keep alive for you many survivors. So it was not you who sent me here, but God; he has made me a father to Pharaoh, and lord of all his house and ruler over all the land of Egypt

Genesis 50:19-20 But Joseph said to them, "Do not be afraid! Am I in the place of God? Even though you intended to do harm to me, God intended it for good, in order to preserve a numerous people, as he is doing today.

It sounds like Joseph was thankful for his painful experiences! God's redemption touches everything. People who've been wronged and suffered greatly often end up carrying deliverance and facilitating change for others who are oppressed, as Joseph did. God is able to turn these wrongs around not only for your good, but also for the good of many others.

Romans 8:28 We know that all things work together for good for those who love God, who are called according to his purpose.

God doesn't plan evil. Men living outside of relationship with God do evil. God does, however, turn around what was meant for evil, and use it for good. Didn't Satan enter Judas and incite him to betray Jesus? Didn't Satan incite the crowds to crucify Jesus? Yet we thank God that Jesus was crucified! If Satan had known the end result, he wouldn't have wanted Jesus sacrificed!

1 Corinthians 2:7-10 But we speak God's wisdom, secret and hidden, which God decreed before the ages for our glory. None of the rulers of this age understood this; for if they had, they would not have crucified the Lord of glory. But, as it is written,
> *"What no eye has seen, nor ear heard, nor the human heart conceived, what God has prepared for those who love him"—these things God has revealed to us through the Spirit.*

When we learn to thank God at all times and for everything, we obtain a heavenly perspective. We see as heavenly people and cooperate with the Holy Spirit so that even what was meant for evil against us, turns out for our good.

When we continually praise and thank the Lord, we turn the eyes of our hearts towards him and behold his glory. We become aware of what the Holy Spirit is doing, so we can partner with him continually. We learn to walk in heavenly reality and have a heavenly perspective. We experience heaven even when hell is all around us, as we see that the earth is full of the glory of the Lord.

These thoughts are challenging. Yet Christians who have gone before us learned to give thanks and praise to God in the direst of circumstances.

Richard Wurmbrand wrote of a man he led to Jesus. The man left behind his wife and six children, who were now starving, when the Communists put him in prison for his Christian faith. He might never see his family again. He was in the same prison cell as Wurmbrand.

Wurmbrand asked if this man felt any resentment against him for leading him to Christ, and because of his family's misery. The man responded *"I have no words to express my thankfulness that you have brought me to the wonderful Savior. I would never have it any other way."*[43]

What a statement! This man lost everything, but had no words to express his gratitude. Such is the joy of salvation, if we really understand it! It is truly a *"joy unspeakable."*[44]

---

[43] Wurmbrand, Richard (2010-09-30). Tortured for Christ (Kindle Locations 511-515). Living Sacrifice Book Company. Kindle Edition.
[44] 1 Peter 1:8 KJV

More Lessons From The Ten Boom Family

The Ten Boom children learned an important lesson from their mother about thankfulness. It was put to the test later when Mr. Ten Boom died in prison, and Corrie and Betsie were taken to a concentration camp. Listen to some wise words from Mrs. Ten Boom.

I glanced out Mama's single window at the brick wall three feet away. "Mama," I said as I set the tray on the bed and sat down beside it, "can't we do something for Tante Bep? I mean, isn't it sad that she has to spend her last days here where she hates it, instead of where she was so happy? The Wallers' or someplace?"

Mama laid down her pen and looked at me. "Corrie," she said at last, "Bep has been just as happy here with us— no more and no less— than she was anywhere else." I stared at her, not understanding. "Do you know when she started praising the Wallers so highly?" Mama went on. "The day she left them. As long as she was there, she had nothing but complaints.

The Wallers couldn't compare with the van Hooks where she'd been before. But at the van Hooks she'd actually been miserable. Happiness isn't something that depends on our surroundings, Corrie. It's something we make inside ourselves."[45]

This is so true! If we wait for circumstances to change before we can be happy, happiness will never come. We sometimes think many things in our lives need to change, but we don't realize the thing needing to change the most is our perspective.

I must remind myself that because I have Christ, I am immeasurably rich. Any afflictions I experience are

---

[45] Boom, Corrie Ten; Elizabeth Sherrill; John Sherrill (2006-01-01). The Hiding Place (p. 49). Baker Publishing Group. Kindle Edition.

"light and temporary" in comparison with the glory before me. Even whatever was meant for my evil will turn out for my good. I can't lose with Christ! I have every reason to rejoice!

Proverbs 15:15 (AMPC) All the days of the desponding and afflicted are made evil [by anxious thoughts and forebodings], but he who has a glad heart has a continual feast [regardless of circumstances].

Listen to what Betsie Ten Boom said as she was being stuffed into a boxcar like an animal for an almost four-day ride to a concentration camp. People were fainting, but were crammed in so tightly they remained upright.

"Do you know what I am thankful for?" Betsie's gentle voice startled me in that squirming madhouse. "I am thankful that Father is in heaven today!"[46]

Many people died in such train rides from suffocation, dehydration, or other causes. There was no sanitation on the train Betsie and Corrie rode on. People sat in their own filth. There was little food or water for the trip. Yet Betsie continued to sing to the Lord as they arrived at the concentration camp after this long train ride.

"The night is dark and I am far from home . . ." Betsie's sweet soprano was picked up by voices all around us. "Lead Thou me on. . . ."[47]

Betsie's countenance shone with the glory of heaven, even in this terrible place. Nothing could rob her of the

---

[46] Boom, Corrie Ten; Elizabeth Sherrill; John Sherrill (2006-01-01). The Hiding Place (p. 198). Baker Publishing Group. Kindle Edition."
[47] Boom, Corrie Ten; Elizabeth Sherrill; John Sherrill (2006-01-01). The Hiding Place (p. 202). Baker Publishing Group. Kindle Edition.

joy of salvation. When the women were stripped naked for weekly inspection, her sister Corrie remembered that soldiers had also stripped Jesus naked and humiliated him.

I leaned toward Betsie, ahead of me in line. Her shoulder blades stood out sharp and thin beneath her blue-mottled skin. "Betsie, they took His clothes, too." Ahead of me I heard a little gasp. "Oh Corrie. And I never thanked Him. . ."[48]

The Lord spoke to Corrie and Betsie through scripture when they read *"give thanks in all circumstances."* This was the key to living in filthy, crowded barracks filled with fleas.

The deck above us was too close to let us sit up. We lay back, struggling against the nausea that swept over us from the reeking straw. We could hear the women who had arrived with us finding their places.

Suddenly I sat up, striking my head on the cross-slats above. Something had pinched my leg. "Fleas!" I cried. "Betsie, the place is swarming with them!" We scrambled across the intervening platforms, heads low to avoid another bump, dropped down to the aisle, and edged our way to a patch of light. "Here! And here another one!" I wailed. "Betsie, how can we live in such a place?"

"Show us. Show us how." It was said so matter of factly it took me a second to realize she was praying. More and more the distinction between prayer and the rest of life seemed to be vanishing for Betsie.

---

[48] Boom, Corrie Ten; Elizabeth Sherrill; John Sherrill (2006-01-01). The Hiding Place (p. 207). Baker Publishing Group. Kindle Edition.

"Corrie!" she said excitedly. "He's given us the answer! Before we asked, as He always does! In the Bible this morning. Where was it? Read that part again!"

I glanced down the long dim aisle to make sure no guard was in sight, then drew the Bible from its pouch. "It was in First Thessalonians," I said.

We were on our third complete reading of the New Testament since leaving Scheveningen. In the feeble light I turned the pages. "Here it is: 'Comfort the frightened, help the weak, be patient with everyone. See that none of you repays evil for evil, but always seek to do good to one another and to all. . . .'" It seemed written expressly to Ravensbrück.

"Go on," said Betsie. "That wasn't all." "Oh yes: '. . . to one another and to all. Rejoice always, pray constantly, give thanks in all circumstances; for this is the will of God in Christ Jesus—'"

"That's it, Corrie! That's His answer. 'Give thanks in all circumstances!' That's what we can do. We can start right now to thank God for every single thing about this new barracks!"

I stared at her, then around me at the dark, foul-aired room. "Such as?" I said.

"Such as being assigned here together." I bit my lip. "Oh yes, Lord Jesus!" "Such as what you're holding in your hands."

I looked down at the Bible. "Yes! Thank You, dear Lord, that there was no inspection when we entered here! Thank You for all the women, here in this room, who will meet You in these pages."

"Yes," said Betsie. "Thank You for the very crowding here. Since we're packed so close, that many more will hear!" She looked at me expectantly. "Corrie!" she prodded.

"Oh, all right. Thank You for the jammed, crammed, stuffed, packed, suffocating crowds."

"Thank You," Betsie went on serenely, "for the fleas and for—"

The fleas! This was too much. "Betsie, there's no way even God can make me grateful for a flea."

"' Give thanks in all circumstances,'" she quoted. "It doesn't say, 'in pleasant circumstances.' Fleas are part of this place where God has put us." And so we stood between piers of bunks and gave thanks for fleas.

But this time I was sure Betsie was wrong.[49]

To Corrie, thanking God for the fleas seemed like too much. But they wondered why the guards didn't bother them in the barracks. They had so much freedom.

Then they realized why. The guards would not enter because of the fleas! This allowed them to freely minister to the other women in the barracks and to read their smuggled Bible.

And thus began the closest, most joyous weeks of all the time in Ravensbrück. Side by side, in the sanctuary of God's fleas, Betsie and I ministered the Word of God to all in the room. We sat by deathbeds that became doorways of heaven. We watched women who had lost everything grow rich in hope.

The knitters of Barracks 28 became the praying heart of the vast diseased body that was Ravensbrück, interceding for all in the camp— guards, under Betsie's prodding, as well as prisoners. We prayed beyond the

---

[49] Boom, Corrie Ten; Elizabeth Sherrill; John Sherrill (2006-01-01). The Hiding Place (p. 209-210). Baker Publishing Group. Kindle Edition.

concrete walls for the healing of Germany, of Europe, of the world—[50]

Betsie turned the eyes of her heart to the Lord as she resolved to *"give thanks in everything,"* and even to thank God for the fleas. She saw that even these barracks were filled with the glory of God. She chose to awaken the dawn, even in Ravensbrück .

She was not repelled by the room as I was. To her it was simply a setting in which to talk about Jesus— as indeed was every place else. Wherever she was, at work, in the food line, in the dormitory, Betsie spoke to those around her about His nearness and His yearning to come into their lives.[51]

In *Present Access To Heaven*, I shared the visions Betsie had in which she saw a house and also a whole concentration camp given them to bring healing and teach forgiveness to holocaust survivors. Betsie told Corrie they would be released before New Year's day.

Betsie didn't survive until then, but everything happened as she had said. Corrie was miraculously released, due to a *"mistake,"* before the New Year. A house and concentration camp exactly like the ones in Betsie's vision were donated as places of healing and recovery. They tore down the fences around the concentration camp and put flower-boxes in the windows of the barracks.

Because Betsie saw the Lord's glory filling a concentration camp, a concentration camp became a

---

[50] Boom, Corrie Ten; Elizabeth Sherrill; John Sherrill (2006-01-01). The Hiding Place (p. 222). Baker Publishing Group. Kindle Edition.
[51] Boom, Corrie Ten; Elizabeth Sherrill; John Sherrill (2006-01-01). The Hiding Place (p. 216). Baker Publishing Group. Kindle Edition.

place dedicated to healing people instead of destroying them!

Does It Really Work?

I know how difficult it is to learn to thank God in everything. This challenges me, just as it challenges you. That's why we have the Holy Spirit to help us!

Though it may be unpleasant to talk about things like a concentration camp, these kinds of stories are evidence that the truths I see in scripture aren't impractical theories. They have been proven in the most extreme circumstances. This encourages me.

The principles I've shared from scripture are powerful and glorious. It's easy to understand how they may be met with skepticism.

Since the whole earth is full of God's glory, any place we are is heaven if the eyes of our hearts are opened. Then as we declare God's praise we *"awaken the dawn"* so others' eyes are opened to the light of the knowledge of the glory of God. This is how nations will come to our light. It's how the earth will be filled with the light of the knowledge of God's glory so nobody will harm or destroy any more.

Is this really possible? My experiences in Belize and other places demonstrated these principles on a small scale. Remarkable testimonies like those of Betsie Ten Boom confirm to me that they really do work!

We looked at the promise of Psalm 84, that those who are always praising the Lord will turn the valley of weeping into a place of springs. I can think of few better examples of a valley of weeping turned into a place of springs, than an entire concentration camp transformed into a place of healing and restoration, where people are taught to love.

If this was the result of one person like Betsie seeing the Lord's glory fill a concentration camp and declaring God's praise, how much more can our cities and nations be transformed?

This is real, so let's get radical about it. Let's get serious about giving thanks to God and declaring his praise in everything. Let's ask the Lord to open the eyes of our hearts so we can see that his glory fills the earth, and so everything around us become heaven to us. Let's awaken the dawn!

10. Ask The Lord For Rain!

Scriptures Triggering Miracles

We've seen that God accomplishes his will through his word, and angels respond when we speak God's word with faith. We can proclaim God's word verbally and nonverbally. When our souls bless the Lord, we radiate light.

This story is about supernatural signs the Lord gave me and my friends to encourage us to pray. It illustrates the principles of proclamation we've discussed. Simply thinking about certain scriptures seemed to be what triggered these supernatural events.

One day I was going to work on a siding job, and on the way I saw a Kay Jewelers sign by the highway saying *"Pray for Rain! (Your ring might be free)."* I knew this wasn't intended to refer to anything scriptural or religious. It was just an advertisement.

Later I discovered it was a promotion. If there was a certain amount of rain on your wedding day, your ring would be free. But what I read on the sign, *"Pray for rain,"* stuck in my mind. All day long I thought of scriptures telling us to ask the Lord for rain. These three passages kept running through my mind as I installed siding:

Hosea 6:3 Let us know, let us press on to know the Lord; his appearing is as sure as the dawn; he will come to us like the showers, like the spring rains that water the earth."

Zechariah 10:1 Ask rain from the Lord in the season of the spring rain, from the Lord who makes the storm clouds, who gives showers of rain to you, the vegetation in the field to everyone.

James 5:16-18 The prayer of a righteous person is powerful and effective. Elijah was a human being, even as we are. He prayed earnestly that it would not rain, and it did not rain on the land for three and a half years. Again he prayed, and the heavens gave rain, and the earth produced its crops.

Supernatural Rain In My House

At that time a friend was staying with me who'd previously been involved in witchcraft but had become a Christian. A few different people lived with me after I bought my first house, in exchange for their help to fix it up.

When I got home from work my housemate told me he just had an encounter with God like he'd never experienced before. He'd been working in the house and praying. He felt like he needed a lot of answers from God, and was listening to a worship song about asking God for rain. He began to cry out *"God send your rain in my life"* and it literally started to rain in the house.

I asked him more about what the experience was like. He said he physically felt rain falling on him and saw it with his eyes open. Later, when he had doubts about his faith, he remembered that.

I was amazed because I had been thinking all day long about the scriptures telling us to pray for rain. I went to the youth meeting that night and the first two worship songs were *"Let it Rain"* by Michael W. Smith and *"Rain Down"* by Delirious.

It was marvelous that I'd been thinking about these scriptures all day, then my friend had this experience in my house, and then the worship songs at youth group were also about rain. This made it clear that God was pointing us to these scriptures about prayer, and saying, *"It's true!"*

John 16:23-24 If you ask anything of the Father in my name, he will give it to you...Ask and you will receive, so that your joy may be complete!

James 4:2 You do not have, because you do not ask

1 John 5:14-15 (NIV) This is the confidence we have in approaching God: that if we ask anything according to his will, he hears us. And if we know that he hears us— whatever we ask—we know that we have what we asked of him.

Elijah Prayed, And It Did Not Rain...

Sometime later my mom witnessed another supernatural occurrence with rain. She was at a Jesuit retreat center to have some time alone with the Lord, and was by herself in a rest area with wooden benches.

The sky got dark, and the storm clouds rolled in. She thought to herself, *"Oh, I really need to be here and pray! I know God can make it not rain on me. If he wants he could put an invisible umbrella over me, but even if it rains and I get soaking wet, I'm going to stay right here, because I need to pray!"*

So she stayed and gave her full attention to the Lord. She says:

It got dark with clouds. I saw the wind billowing in the trees to my right and heard raindrops spatter against the leaves. The farmer's field in front of me was also pitter pattering with raindrops. Soon there were puddles on the bench to my left.

Yet I did not get wet! There was a dry circle around me, as if there truly had been an invisible umbrella. I reached my hand outside the perimeter of the circle and felt raindrops, then pulled it back in, where there was no rain at all. By the time the rain stopped I'd had a wonderful time of fellowship with the Lord.

I walked back to my dorm completely dry on a rain soaked path through woods still dripping from the downpour. What especially amazed me was that I had not even prayed, either audibly or silently, but the Lord heard my unspoken thoughts and met me at my point of faith, granting my heart's desire."

I have experienced the power of God working before with only a thought. In fact, I was born again and delivered from oppression when I had the God-inspired thought *"What is there to be depressed about?"*

These supernatural experiences with rain pointed us to what scripture says about Elijah. He was a man like us, but he prayed, and it did not rain for three and a half years. He prayed again, and it rained.

These signs from God led me to meditate on many scriptures about prayer and to share the scriptures and testimonies with others. God was telling us he wants us to ask, he wants us to believe, and we need to pray for rain. This was how he renewed my focus on scriptures concerning prayer.

Ask God for rain! *"Whatever you ask for in prayer, believe that you have received it, and it will be yours."*[52] God will send rain if you ask! God wants to pour out his rain in abundance on you, on your family,

---

[52] Mark 11:24, NRSV

on your city, and on your country. He will if you ask and believe!

God's Rain

Sometimes we may ask God for physical rain, especially in a time of drought. However, rain is also symbolic in scripture of refreshment and of God's goodness and blessing.

Matthew 6:44-46 But I tell you, love your enemies and pray for those who persecute you, that you may be children of your Father in heaven. He causes his sun to rise on the evil and the good, and sends rain on the righteous and the unrighteous. If you love those who love you, what reward will you get? Are not even the tax collectors doing that?

Isaiah 45:8 "You heavens above, rain down my righteousness; let the clouds shower it down. Let the earth open wide, let salvation spring up, let righteousness flourish with it; I, the Lord, have created it.

Isaiah 55:10-11 As the rain and the snow come down from heaven, and do not return to it without watering the earth and making it bud and flourish, so that it yields seed for the sower and bread for the eater, so is my word that goes out from my mouth: It will not return to me empty, but will accomplish what I desire and achieve the purpose for which I sent it.

The Prayer Of Faith

Here's a larger portion of James chapter five, which gives context to the scripture about Elijah praying for rain. The context here is the prayer of faith for the sick.

James 5:14-18 Are any among you sick? They should call for the elders of the church and have them pray over them, anointing them with oil in the name of the Lord. The prayer of faith will save the sick, and the Lord will raise them up; and anyone who has committed sins will be forgiven.

Therefore confess your sins to one another, and pray for one another, so that you may be healed. The prayer of the righteous is powerful and effective. Elijah was a human being like us, and he prayed fervently that it might not rain, and for three years and six months it did not rain on the earth. Then he prayed again, and the heaven gave rain and the earth yielded its harvest.

A Man Just Like Us

James says Elijah was a man like us. Often we may feel like we don't have the same super-human kind of faith Elijah and other great *"men of God"* had. However, these people had the same weaknesses we have. They weren't super-humans. Even Jesus was tempted in every way as we are.[53]

God brought strength out of their weakness, and he can do the same for you! I remember when I first witnessed healing miracles. I was convinced God wanted to heal people, but I felt like I was too weak and discouraged to believe. I felt like my faith was a failure.

Even so, I believed God could do the impossible thing of bringing me to a place of faith to believe for people to be healed. He brought power out of my weakness, and I began to see miracles happen sooner than I expected!

---

[53] Hebrews 4:15

God can do what you can't! He can work faith in you even though you feel powerless to believe! In fact, he promises to work in you, enabling you to will and to work for His good pleasure![54]

The Story Of Elijah

James 5 is the only place where the New Testament commands us to pray for the sick. Although we often talk about praying for the sick, we don't read about Jesus praying for the sick in scripture. Jesus did pray — sometimes he stayed up praying all night. However, when he encountered the sick, he healed them.

Jesus never commanded his disciples to pray for the sick either. He commanded them to lay hands on the sick, anoint them with oil, cast out demons, and heal them. Let's go back to look at the story of Elijah in First Kings 17 and 18, to which James is referring. We see from this story that the prayer of faith is accompanied by action and declaration.

1 Kings 17:1 Now Elijah the Tishbite, of Tishbe in Gilead, said to Ahab, "As the Lord the God of Israel lives, before whom I stand, there shall be neither dew nor rain these years, except by my word."

James says Elijah prayed and it did not rain for three and a half years. When we read the story in First Kings we see that Elijah did not only pray; he boldly declared God's word. After this, God supernaturally provided for Elijah during the drought. We read of that provision in the rest of chapter 17.

1 Kings 18:1-2 After many days the word of the Lord came to Elijah, in the third year of the drought, saying,

---

[54] Philippians 2:13

"Go, present yourself to Ahab; I will send rain on the earth." So Elijah went to present himself to Ahab.

Following this, we read of the confrontation between Elijah and the prophets of Baal, where God answered by fire and consumed not only Elijah's sacrifice, but the wood, the stones, the dust, and the water in the trench around it. After that the nation turned to God and they killed the prophets of Baal. Then...

1 Kings 18:41 Elijah said to Ahab, "Go up, eat and drink; for there is a sound of rushing rain."

There was still no natural sign of rain. Elijah heard the sound of a rushing rain by faith, because God spoke to him. Before he even prayed, Elijah declared God's word as fact. Romans 4:17(ASV) says God *"giveth life to the dead, and calleth the things that are not, as though they were."*

God has given us the same spirit of faith so that as he does, we will call things that are not as though they were.

2 Corinthians 4:13 we have the same spirit of faith that is in accordance with scripture—"I believed, and so I spoke"—we also believe, and so we speak...

Elijah's prayer of faith involved calling things that were not as though they were. Every natural sign showed any possibility of rain was *"dead."* But Elijah spoke as a fact *"there is a sound of rushing rain."* He said it before there was any natural way to sense rain. What he spoke was not based on physical senses but on God's word.

1 Kings 18:42-46 So Ahab went up to eat and to drink. Elijah went up to the top of Carmel; there he bowed himself down upon the earth and put his face between his knees.

He said to his servant, "Go up now, look toward the sea." He went up and looked, and said, "There is nothing." Then he said, "Go again seven times." At the seventh time he said, "Look, a little cloud no bigger than a person's hand is rising out of the sea."

Then he said, "Go say to Ahab, 'Harness your chariot and go down before the rain stops you.'" In a little while the heavens grew black with clouds and wind; there was a heavy rain.

Ahab rode off and went to Jezreel. But the hand of the Lord was on Elijah; he girded up his loins and ran in front of Ahab to the entrance of Jezreel.

Again, Elijah did not pay attention to what his natural senses said, but to God's word. When there was no natural sign of rain, he sent the servant to look again. As soon as there was the slightest natural sign of rain, Elijah declared *"go down before the rain stops you!"* Elijah declared what would happen according to the word of the Lord both before and after he prayed. This is what the prayer of faith looks like. Consider the following scriptures:

James 1:6 (KJV) But let him ask in faith, nothing wavering. For he that wavereth is like a wave of the sea driven with the wind and tossed.

1 Corinthians 15:58 (NIV) Therefore, my dear brothers and sisters, stand firm. Let nothing move you.

Ephesians 6:13-14 (NIV) Therefore put on the full armor of God, so that when the day of evil comes, you may be able to stand your ground, and after you have done everything, to stand. Stand firm then, with the belt of truth buckled around your waist...

Stand Firm!

This is what the prayer of faith looks like. It calls what is not as though it were, according to the word of the Lord. It declares, and continues to pray and expect, even when there's no natural sign of fulfillment. As soon as a little sign of rain appears, faith rejoices and declares God's word again. Elijah stood firm on God's word, not wavering even when there was no natural sign of anything coming to pass.

The prayer of faith is prayer with thanksgiving. Like Elijah did, we thank God for the answer before we see it naturally. As we give praise to God, it becomes a fact to us.

Psalm 66:16-17 (ESV) Come and hear, all you who fear God, and I will tell what he has done for my soul. I cried to him with my mouth, and high praise was on my tongue.

When I first got into healing, I often gave up too soon when I laid my hands on a person and they didn't immediately feel anything. However, the more I continued ministering to people, the more my faith grew. I knew and felt a heavenly reality in my spirit even when there was no natural sign. I could feel the Holy Spirit's power flowing through me and knew God's word was reality, even when the person didn't yet feel any difference.

I remember when a man asked me to pray for his wife. She had large and painful ovarian cysts. I could see the pain on her face. I put my hand behind her back and commanded them to be gone. She didn't feel any change, but I knew God's word was true. I felt the peace of God around me.

I proclaimed God's word again. I asked if she felt anything. She said no. I prayed in faith again, waited and asked again. This happened several times. It was like Elijah telling his servant to go look for a sign of rain, but he saw nothing.

For ten minutes she felt nothing. Before, I would have given up by then. However, I had grown in Christ and been strengthened in my innermost being by the Holy Spirit. So I continued, full of the peace of God, feeling grace exploding from my heart.

Then after ten minutes, she felt a little bit of heat in her ovaries. Yay! I rejoiced like Elijah did when a little cloud the size of a man's hand came from the sea. Just a little sign, and he said *"Go down before the rain stops you!"* Just a little sign, and I said, *"Yay! You are being healed."*

When I thanked God the heat increased until soon there was no more pain or tenderness. The cysts were gone, and she didn't need surgery! Thank you God for your rain!

You might be a weak human being like Elijah, who was a man like us. But the spirit of Christ dwells in you, if you are his! God will work faith in you and enable you to believe if you say yes and cry out *"God, I want your rain!"* God, *"I believe; help my unbelief!"*[55]

The context in James 5 shows us how praying for rain relates to the prayer of faith for healing. We see that though it is the only place the Bible commands us to pray for the sick, declaration and action in faith are also involved.

Nations Will Turn To The Light Of The Lord

The story in First Kings shows us that asking for God's rain is also about having faith for our nations to be saved.

---

[55] Mark 9:24

Elijah was a man like us, and he led a nation to reject Baal and return to the Lord. Get your eyes off of your weaknesses and failures, and remember that if God could do such a thing with a man like Elijah, he can do it with you!

Revelation 11:15 The kingdom of the world has become the kingdom of our Lord and of his Messiah

Habakkuk 2:14 But the earth will be filled with the knowledge of the glory of the Lord, as the waters cover the sea.

Many of us have, at times, felt frustrated with prayer. Many Christians have become disillusioned with prayer movements that taught them to pray ineffectually, in unbelief. In the first book of this series, we saw ways we can pray fervently but in unbelief, not realizing we deny the gospel in our very prayers.

I want to encourage you, as the Lord has encouraged me! Remember God's promises. Scripture exhorts us to not let ourselves be discouraged with prayer, but to persevere.

Ephesians 6:18 Pray in the Spirit at all times in every prayer and supplication. To that end keep alert and always persevere in supplication for all the saints.

Luke 18:1 (NIV) Then Jesus told his disciples a parable to show them that they should always pray and not give up.

In the early 90's, a series of prayer initiatives began which encouraged people to pray for the countries and people in the 10/40 window. The 10/40 window is an area of the world in which most of the people groups that have never heard the gospel live.

Since then, people in these countries have been coming to the Lord in numbers greater than ever before in the history of the world. Many Muslims are having dreams and visions of Jesus and being converted. Previously unreached people groups have embraced the gospel. The prayer of faith works! Prayer with thanksgiving and declaration can change nations!

Psalm 102:15 The nations will fear the name of the LORD, and all the kings of the earth your glory.

Psalm 138:4-5 All the kings of the earth shall praise you, O LORD, for they have heard the words of your mouth. They shall sing of the ways of the LORD, for great is the glory of the LORD.

Whether it's asking for God's rain of blessing on your life, praying the prayer of faith for the sick, or asking God to bring salvation to your city or nation, ask God for rain now! Ask and believe he wants to pour out his blessing on you, and he will do it!

Yes, the nations can be saved! Ask the Lord to pour out his rain on your country; then declare it! Declare God's rain will fall on your family, in your sphere of influence, and on whoever enters your house. Believe they will tangibly experience the glory of God.

Ask God for rain, and he will send his rain! Expect people to be healed, to feel God's peace, and to be delivered from oppression when they walk in the door of your house. In fact, why not pray and believe people will be healed, delivered, and feel God's peace even as they walk by your house on the street?

John 11:40 "Did I not tell you that if you believed, you would see the glory of God?"

If you believe, you will see God's glory! This is why God gave us these signs — so we remember these scriptures and believe they are true!

May You Awaken The Dawn!

Maybe what you've read in this book challenges you. How can you praise the Lord and give thanks in everything? Breaking patterns of negative thinking and complaining, which hinder you from seeing what the Holy Spirit is doing, may seem too difficult. How can you see your surroundings as heaven? It challenges me too!

But God has given us the Holy Spirit to empower us to do what's impossible with merely human ability. So on we go! As you break bad habits and make new ones, it will become easier.

I remember sleeping with a Bible under my pillow when I was a child, so I would remember to read it the next day. As you ask the Holy Spirit to help you walk as a heavenly person, I encourage you to do something to remind yourself to give thanks to the *Lord.*

I wrote Psalm 34:8 *"I will bless the Lord at all times; His praise shall continually be in my mouth"* on my wall in permanent marker. Maybe you can't write on your wall or you rent an apartment, but you can find ways to establish a habit of giving thanks to the Lord.

Psalm 63:5 My soul is satisfied as with a rich feast, and my mouth praises you with joyful lips

It's a good idea to make a written record of the ways the Lord has helped you and delivered you in the past. Remind yourself what the Lord has done for you. Lately,

Facebook has been reminding me of miracles the Lord has done in my past. It brings up things I posted a few years ago on the same date, and often reminds me of miracles I had forgotten.

You can also search for websites that have testimonies, and make a habit of regularly reading and talking about testimonies of what the Lord has done. As you step out to bless others, laying hands on people and proclaiming God's word, you will have more testimonies of your own to share.

I pray the Lord would open the eyes of your heart and give you a heavenly perspective. In Jesus' name, I pray you would start seeing angels and become constantly aware of what the Holy Spirit is doing in every situation, so you can partner with him.

May you become so aware of the Lord's presence and glory filling the earth around you, that every place you go is heaven to you. May you learn to always draw water from the wells of salvation and proclaim the Lord's mighty works. May your mouth be filled with glad shouts of salvation and joy! May you be surrounded with glad cries of salvation as people around you are set free!

May your soul bless the Lord until your whole being radiates light. May you do exploits as you grow strong in faith, giving thanks to God. Like Elijah, may you pray prayers that change nations. Let it rain! May the mountains standing before you melt like wax from the heat of the manifestation of God's presence, as you declare his glory!

May you awaken the dawn, until the whole earth is full of the knowledge of the glory of the Lord, as the waters cover the seas!

About The Author

Jonathan Brenneman was born in Rochester, New York and raised in Pennsylvania. Although a very troubled child he was at the same time very religious. He read the Bible from cover to cover when he was seven years old, all the while questioning and wondering about the existence of God.

When Jonathan was nine years old, he woke up one morning with bad back pain. His mother prayed for him, and to his surprise, he felt something like a hot ball of energy rolling up and down inside his back, and the pain melted away. It was shocking to say the least, but it convinced him God did exist! He later told his friends, "I know that God is real. I felt his hand on my back."

In spite of this experience, Jonathan still had no peace. He prayed the "sinner's prayer" but with no change until two years later when he had a "born again" experience. It felt like heaven opened and unexplainable joy and peace descended upon him! He was different, and knew it! The things he had felt so guilty about that he tried unsuccessfully to change, were simply gone.

After this time, Jonathan dedicated his life to the Lord as a missionary, going on his first mission trip at age fourteen. As a teenager and young adult he continued to travel and learn languages. Then, when he was twenty-one and during a time of desperation, Jonathan went to a Christian conference where he was very encouraged and touched by the Lord. It was a start of a supernatural lifestyle and growing in spiritual gifts during which time many amazing miracles and healings began to happen.

Jonathan worked in construction, but in between jobs he began to visit churches in the United States and Canada as well as in Latin America and Eastern Europe. His ministry journeys have included Russia, Ukraine,

Poland, Italy, Canada, Mexico, Belize, and Brazil. In these places Jonathan has encouraged the believers and shared testimonies, and spoken with unbelievers and prayed for them. He also worked with children and seniors. He dedicated a lot of time to talking with, praying for, and encouraging people wherever he went, all the while growing in an experience of a love for people that is beyond understanding—for it is God's love. Jonathan believes it is a wonderful and tremendous privilege to be able to serve the people for whom Jesus gave his life.

Jonathan is now a missionary in Rio de Janeiro Brazil with his wife Elizabeth, and daughter Rebekah. He loves people, enjoys being with them, and rejoices at seeing what the Holy Spirit does in their lives. He likes to minister in the role of teaching, laying hands on the sick, visiting the elderly, and working with children— always loving them so they in turn will learn to love others with the love of God.

Contact

You can get in touch with Jonathan through his blog at www.gotoheavennow.com, at Goodreads, or through his Facebook author page, *Jonathan Brenneman.*

Amazon reviews are the author's tip jar! They also help to get the message out to more people. If you have enjoyed this book, please consider leaving a review on Goodreads and/or Amazon.com.

Also By Jonathan Brenneman

Of The "Heaven Now" Series
Part 1: Present Access To Heaven

Present Access to Heaven presents a strong scriptural foundation for Christians to experience heaven while on earth, regardless of earthly circumstances. This book expounds on the unspeakably glorious riches that are available to every believer. It deals with subtle mindsets which undermine the truth of the gospel and hinder us from living fully in the reality accessible through Christ.

Because the truths shared may seem "too good to be true," *Present Access to Heaven* is filled with true stories, illustrating that these are not just theories but real possibilities for every believer. This book is loaded with encouragement and will challenge you to come into an experiential knowledge of the Lord's goodness as never before!

JONATHAN BRENNEMAN

——— PRESENT ———

ACCESS

TOHEAVEN

HEAVEN NOW SERIES PART 1

Part 3: Jesus Has Come In The Flesh

The Apostle John taught that every spirit confessing Jesus has come in the flesh is from God, and every spirit that does not confess Jesus is not from God, but is antichrist. (1 John 4:2-3) *Jesus Has Come In The Flesh* expounds on the implications of Jesus coming from heaven to live in an earthly human body. Understanding this truth can be used to test any spirit or teaching to see whether or not it is from God.

The influence of a spirit that denies Jesus has come in the flesh can be linked to every major problem in our societies, including sexual immorality, poverty, and violence. Learn to recognize the lies of the antichrist spirit which have infiltrated the church, and to root out the influence of the antichrist spirit from your thinking.

A spirit that denies Christ has come in the flesh opposes the tangible anointing of God's power and glory. Understanding the truth that Jesus has come in the flesh will cause you to walk in Holy Spirit anointing to bring about greater manifestations of God's power and glory in and through your life.

You will see how ministering physical healing demonstrates Jesus has come in the flesh; undoing the work of the devil and opposing the demonic onslaught of sexual immorality and violence in our societies. Read how the truths in *Jesus Has Come In The Flesh* have changed my life!

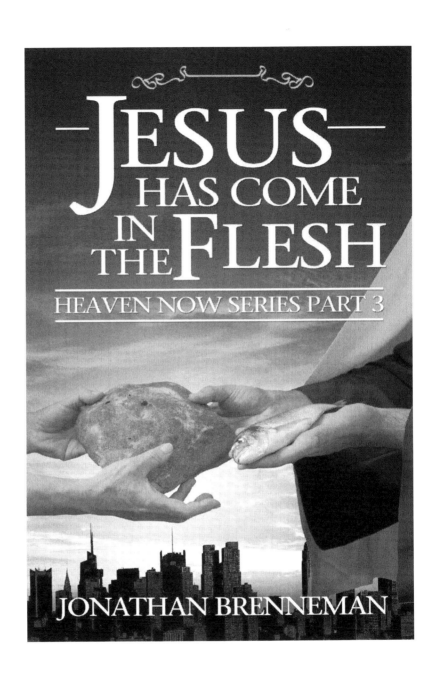

I Am Persuaded

Christian Leadership As Taught By Jesus

"Jonathan Brenneman in his *I Am Persuaded* provokes, jabs and challenges our sacred cows of church leadership. Yet, the jabs are not hurtful because they come from Scripture. This is not a reactionary book filled with leader bashing but a graceful and excellent presentation of mostly forgotten principles concerning how Jesus and the early church taught and practiced leadership.

All the key and at times controversial words are discussed: rule, obey, submission, apostles, authority, and spiritual covering. Excellent exegesis on these words is provided and is foundational to the author's conclusions. If you find yourself disagreeing, then, by all means, do a better exegesis. I think that will be difficult. Jonathan Brenneman has personally made a paradigm shift in his life and shares it with us. Will you?

I Am Persuaded is more than a fine Bible study, it is filled with real life stories which illustrate servant leadership. It is well written, fast paced, and provokes fresh thinking. I believe the reader and the church will be healthier when these principles are put into practice. Will you be persuaded? Will you undergo a paradigm shift? Read and find out. This is a good book and its message needs to be heard."

DR. STAN NEWTON—*Missionary in Bulgaria; Author: Glorious Kingdom.*

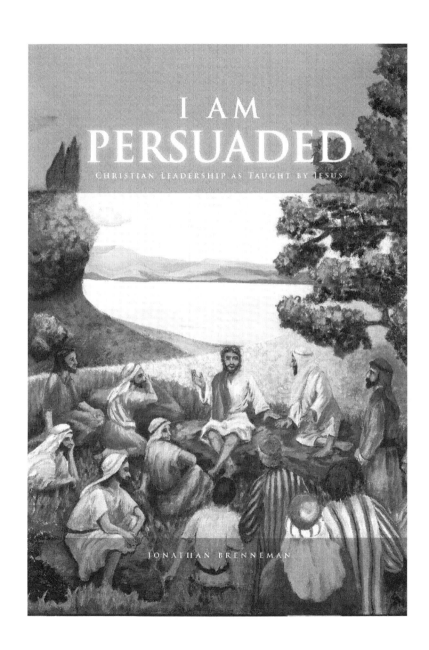

I AM
PERSUADED

CHRISTIAN LEADERSHIP AS TAUGHT BY JESUS

JONATHAN BRENNEMAN

The Power-And-Love Sandwich

Why You Should Seek God's Face AND His Hand

If you've started to step out in the supernatural things of God, it's likely that may have found yourself on the receiving end of a great deal of opposition. While you may have anticipated that those closest to you would be supportive and encouraging, instead your testimonies may have been met with a backlash. Fellow believers may have suggested that your focus on spiritual gifts is unbalanced. It may have been said that you're too preoccupied with signs and wonders.

In Jonathan Brenneman's book *The Power And Love Sandwich*, he explores the theological position of seeking God's face in conjunction with seeking His hand. Jonathan puts things into perspective and helps us to see through scripture that we don't have to pick one or the other. Both are liberally and unapologetically available to us. We can simultaneously embrace both the power of God and the love of God without having to forego one in order to embrace the other.

This book is a must read for those who intend to move in the power and love of God. You will learn to confidently walk in both the fruit of the Spirit as well as the gifts of the Spirit. The misguided objections of well-intended believers won't have the same power to break your spirit. Instead you will learn to shake it off, love them despite their opposition and remain kingdom focused.

CHERYL FRITZ—Founder
Inside Out Training and Equipping School

THE POWER & LOVE SANDWICH

Why You Should Seek Gods Face AND His Hand

Jonathan Breneman

Made in the USA
San Bernardino, CA
15 October 2016